FROM MINOR SETBACK TO MAJOR COMEBACK

EVERETTE
WITHERSPOON

FROM MINOR SETBACK TO MAJOR COMEBACK

Print ISBN: 978-1-66783-7-246
eBook ISBN: 978-1-66783-7-253

CONTENTS

INTRODUCTION

In the paper, it was written that my political career was over and that I was done. I laughed when I first heard those statements, but the truth is, more than a year later, the talk, the gossip, and the feedback were true. I am done, excuse my Ebonics, but I done triumphed. I done went to another level. I done written three amazing books. I done reinvented myself. I done made an amazing comeback. I done came back stronger than ever. Most importantly, what God has done in my life is truly spectacular. So, I think I'm done is the best choice of words.

It was written that it was over for me. "Over" is a great choice of words because the truth is I have overcome. And I am truly overwhelmed by the support of my family and friends while I was incarcerated. Most importantly, I am truly overwhelmed by the goodness of God and his blessings. So "over" is the correct word. But although life can only be understood by looking backward, it must be lived by looking forward.

This book is about the future and the steps you must take every day in the present moment to make sure you fulfill your goals, dreams, and destiny. There is a saying that goes, "Tomorrow is a mystery, yesterday is history, all we have is today that's why it's called the present, because every day and every moment is a gift." This book is about the present moment and what you can do to make the most of the present moment to ensure that you have a great future. I believe the rest of our lives is the best of our lives. And no matter what we have gone through, if we do certain things consistently, we will have the strength to overcome obstacles. If we do certain things consistently, we will have the strength to turn our tests into testimonies, our mess into messages, our misery into ministry, and our setbacks into comebacks. In this book, I will show you the things that you need to do consistently to give you the strength to overcome obstacles and ensure your comeback.

There is something in the human spirit that craves a comeback. We crave it in our movies. We crave it in our books. We crave it in our relationships; that's why, we break up to make up. Most importantly, we crave a comeback in our individual lives. Whether it's being fired from your job and wanting to find another one, a better one, or starting your own business and becoming more successful. Whether it's dropping out of school when you are young and in college and returning to school ten years later and obtaining your bachelor's, master's, or PhD while working and raising a family. Whether it's switching from one unfulfilling career to a more rewarding and fulfilling one. Whether it's getting divorced and remarrying the man or woman of your dreams. Whether it's regaining your health and getting into the best shape of your life after a life-threatening illness. Whether it's regaining your happiness after it seems life has taken all your joy. We all crave a comeback.

In prison, I used to always say, "This is a minor setback for a major comeback." One of the inmates asked me, "How can you call this situation a minor setback? We are in prison!" You, the reader, might say just like that inmate. I have just lost my job, I have health issues, I have recently been divorced, my teenage daughter is pregnant, or my son is in jail. "How can you call that minor?" My answer is the same one I gave to my fellow inmate in prison. I told the story about this elderly lady who would pray to God every morning and tell God, "Today, I will handle the small problems; I just need you to handle the big problems in my life." God responded to her by saying, "My child, to me, all things are small." I'm saying to you, as I said to my fellow inmate, that all things are small to God and all things are minor to God. With God, there is no difference between five million dollars and five cents. The issue is our faith and our perspective.

The bigger your faith, the bigger your God will be in your eyes and the smaller your problems will be in your eyes. The smaller your faith, the smaller God will be in your eyes and the bigger your problems will be in your eyes. I can say all my problems are small because God is big in my eyes. In this book, I will show you how to grow and increase your faith before, during, and after trials, so that God will be big in your eyes and problems will become smaller in your eyes.

As a matter of fact, when you have the right perspective, problems and the winds of adversity can help you. Think about the wind. The wind blows out a candle, but it spreads a forest fire. When the winds of adversity come, does it extinguish your fire or does it spread your fire? When you have a small fire, it won't survive the winds of adversity; it will be extinguished. When you have a strong fire, the winds of adversity will spread your fire and turn it into an all-consuming fire that cannot be quenched or extinguished. How great is your fire to start that business? How great is your fire to go back to school and to excel in your career? Does the wind of adversity blow your fire out or does it make you say, "I'm going to become stronger and keep pursing my goals"? In this book, I will show you how to increase your desire so that it becomes a raging fire that cannot be extinguished by the winds of adversity, but instead will be spread by the winds of adversity.

I believe this book will provide you with both excitement and enlightenment, and all that I ask from you, the reader, is that you keep an open mind. As the saying goes, "The mind is like a parachute; it does not work unless it is open." If there are any principles in this book that you do not agree with, I ask that you eat the fruit and spit out the seeds. If there are any ideas or principles that do not apply to you, spit them out like apple seeds because even though you spit the seeds of the apple out, it does not take away from the sweetness of the apple. With that being said, I introduce to you: *From Minor Setback to Major Comeback*.

CHAPTER 1:

THE PROCESS

The first key to turning a minor setback into a major comeback is to not let the process stop your progress. Let me ask you a question: Who is Jesus without Judas? Who is David without Goliath? Who is Moses without Pharaoh, the Egyptian Army, and the Red Sea? Who is Noah without the flood? Who is Daniel without the lion's den? Who is Shadrach, Meshach, and Abednego without the fiery furnace? Who is Martin Luther King Jr. without segregation and racism? Who is Rosa Parks without a segregated bus system? Who is Nelson Mandela without incarceration and apartheid?

Would we even know and remember these great individuals without their tests and trials? Would their lives be written about if these trials would not have come into their life? Would these individuals inspire us and give us courage to go through our everyday struggles if they had not faced such great trials? Why did these trials come into their life? One simple word, process. One of the ugliest words in the world is process, but if you want to turn a minor setback into a major comeback, you must understand that setbacks are part of the process and very few people, if any, fulfill their dreams and reach their goals without encountering setbacks.

When I was a kid, my mother used to wake up early on Saturday mornings and cook a big breakfast with either bacon, sausage, country ham, biscuits, or pancakes. The smell was so delightful and savory that it instantly woke me up from my sleep and had me in a great mood throughout the day. The smell and taste of the breakfast was so good that when I was a kid on Friday nights, I went to bed early anticipating that breakfast just as much as Saturday morning cartoons. What I did not realize in my young, naive mind is that the process the pork had been through to make it so tantalizing to my nose and taste buds was a nasty process. If you have ever had the unfortunate experience of visiting a hog-processing plant, it has the worst odor you will ever smell.

It's the same thing with fried chicken. That fried chicken smells and tastes so good that a lot of people can't even concentrate on what the pastor is preaching about on Sunday morning because their mind is fantasizing about that Sunday dinner, which almost always features fried chicken. Whether it is Popeye's or homemade fried chicken, we love our fried chicken. As a matter of fact, the three things that make Sunday important is church, chicken, and NFL football. The irony is that most of us have never been to a chicken-processing plant. It is nasty, it smells terrible, and there might be rodents and insects around. You have migrant workers who are not paid living wages. It is an ugly process to get that savory chicken to your table.

Just like chicken and pork, we often look at the finished product of people we deem successful, but we do not know about the ugly process. Even in our own lives, we might have a goal, or God might have a plan for our lives, but he does not show us the process. He does not show us the setbacks and heartaches that are part of the process. If he did, we will probably not want to go through with it.

The process can be very painful. Think about processed hair. Processed hair is hair that has been chemically treated during production to make it appear a certain way. Prior to being styled, processed hair is soaked in a highly acidic bath to strip off its cuticles and emit all the natural characteristics of the strands. Basically, the process removes all the naps and curls out of the hair to make it straight. Process in real life is painful, but it straightens us out. What do we do when God puts the spiritual hot comb to our lives to straighten us out? The same concept applies with Processed foods and processed meats. I personally don't like processed foods and meats, but processed meat is any meat which has been modified to improve its taste or to extend its shelf life. God uses process in our life to modify us to make us better, make us last longer, and give us more endurance and perseverance.

When I was first indicted on trumped-up tax charges and sentenced to prison, I was searching for understanding. While sitting in my cell in solitary confinement, a question came to me. *What is the thing a lot of women want more than anything?* The first thing that came to my mind was security. Then from the inside of me, I heard a *no*. What a lot of women want more than anything is to have a child. Then I heard from the inside of me, *what is the most painful thing that the average woman will go through naturally?* I said childbirth. From the inside of me, I heard that just like pregnancy and the experience of giving birth, the most painful things in life will give us what we want the most if we push through it. If a woman is pregnant and she does not push during the painful experience, that child could end up strangling on its umbilical cord and the child could end up stillborn.

The same way, a lot of our dreams have died during the painful process because we did not push in the middle of the process, we just simply gave up because the pain was so great. When you are experiencing a setback, and you are going through the process, it can be a dark time in your life. That's why it is important to understand that there is a difference between the darkness of the tomb and the darkness of the womb. The darkness of the tomb means that you are dead. The darkness of the womb means that something new is about to be born.

From our hard times and setbacks, new dreams can be born. New relationships can be born. New opportunities can be born. New businesses, callings, careers, and insights can be born. Your darkest times and setbacks in your life can lead to the brightest times and biggest comebacks in your life if you push through. There is no pain like a woman giving birth, and there is no joy like the joy of a child being born. The key is that the mother must push through the pain. The thing that often makes us give up in the middle of a setback is that often we feel the pain, but we do not recognize the new opportunities that are in front of us to benefit from and to comeback stronger than ever from that pain.

Take for example a new day. A new day starts at twelve a.m. It is midnight; it is still dark outside, but a new day has arrived. A new day does not start when it is seven in the morning and the sun comes up. It starts when it is still dark; it may be dark in your life, but you have entered a new day. I was indicted; I was in prison; I was under investigation by the FBI and the IRS. It was unfair; it was dark outside, but it was a new day in my life. Even though the sun was not shining, it was still a new day.

You might be in a bad relationship, but it is a new day. You might have been fired from your job, but it's a new day. You might have lost a loved one, but it's a new day. It might be dark in your life; it might be hard right now. You might be in the middle of a setback, but it is a new day. Keep pushing because with every new day, it starts out dark, but eventually the sun shines; just push through the pain.

That's the thing about the process: it is very painful, but all pain is not bad, a lot of pain is good. Some pain is divine. Sometimes when you go to the doctor, the doctor will recommend surgery, and that surgery can be painful. There is a difference between being cut with a knife and being cut with a scalpel from surgery. The cut from the knife is meant to harm or kill you. The cut from the surgeon is meant to heal or save your life. Both the knife and the surgeon's scalpel hurt and are painful. Both the knife and scalpel make you bleed. Both the knife and the scalpel will leave you sore. But the knife is meant to kill you, and the scalpel is meant to save your life. Both the knife and scalpel cause pain; the only difference is the intent of the wielder; the wielder of the knife is using that knife to try to kill you. The wielder of the scalpel is wielding the scalpel to try to heal you.

Divine pain comes into our life to heal us. To get rid of the infections that are in our lives, that are keeping us from being our best, reaching our goals, fulfilling our dreams, and making that major comeback. The process is painful, but it is necessary. Process is something that every person had to go through to be born into this world physically, and process is something that everybody must go through to fulfill their destiny (the reason why they were born).

I heard a story about a kid who grew up in Detroit in the 1930s and 1940s. This kid loved playing baseball. This kid had a dream of playing for the Detroit Tigers one day. This kid was a great baseball player in high school, and after high school, he went away to serve in the military. This kid, when he came back to Detroit in 1952, was now a grown man. The Detroit Tigers offered him a contract to play in the minor leagues. He worked hard every day in practice; his skills improved, and he was about to land a contract with the Detroit Tigers to play on their major league team. Three years into his four-year contract with the minor league team, tragedy struck.

This young man suffered a terrible knee injury that forced him to quit playing baseball. He was depressed and discouraged. His dreams were shattered. He was in the middle of the process, and he was facing a setback. All he ever wanted to do since he was a child was play professional baseball for the Detroit Tigers. Life seemed unfair. He was forced to move back home with his parents. His father reminded the young man that he had told this young man since he was a kid that he would never make it playing baseball, and that he needed to get a real job and stop wasting so much time chasing a dream.

This young man had a friend who owned a restaurant. He asked his friend if he could work for him until he found another job. His friend told him that his restaurant did not have any job openings. The young man said that he did not need to be paid, he just needed somewhere to go during the day so that his father would think that he was working. The owner of the restaurant told the young man that he could go in the back and help make pizzas if he wanted to. The young man started working in the restaurant for free, making pizzas. He became so good at it that he started his own restaurant. His restaurant was so successful that he opened more restaurants. Today everybody has heard of Little Caesars Pizza, the restaurant that the young man started.

I'm sure, at the time, the knee injury was a big disappointment and setback, but it moved him toward his destiny. It was dark in his life when he injured his knee, but it was a new day in his life. It was dark in his life when he hurt his knee, but it was not the darkness of the tomb, it was the darkness of the womb, a new destiny was being born. I'm sure it hurt when his dream of playing baseball came to an end, but it was not the pain of a knife; it was the pain of a scalpel. The man's name is Mike Ilitch. Mike had a dream of playing for the Detroit Tigers, but God had a bigger dream. Because Mike Ilitch's Little Caesars restaurants are so successful, he now owns the Detroit Tigers. Mike had planned on playing for the Detroit Tigers, but God had planned on him owning the Detroit Tigers. The same thing can and will happen to you if you do not let the process stop your progress. Mike Ilitch suffered a minor setback, but, in the end, it ended up becoming a major comeback.

CHAPTER 2:

GET IN THE GAME

The second step to overcoming a setback is to recognize and realize that setbacks will come into your life if you are doing the right thing. Most people think that when hard times or setbacks come into their life, it is because they are doing something wrong. This outlook on life is only partially true. A lot of times, hard times and setbacks come into our lives because we are doing the right things.

Take for instance a football game. During a football game, the defense only tries to tackle the person with the ball. If you are close to scoring a touchdown, the defense is going to do everything they can to give you a setback by tackling you. The defense will try to strip the ball from you. The defense will try to make you fumble the ball to stop you because you are about to score.

Well, you are on God's team, and any time you fulfill your dreams and your God-given destiny, you are scoring points for God's team. If you are experiencing setbacks or have obstacles coming against you and people trying to attack you, it could be because you have the ball and you are about to score. A lot of times when you are on your way to reaching your goals, you will experience a setback and all hell will seem to break loose. This happens to test your persistence, and if you pass the test, you will go to the next level.

The reason the Detroit Pistons were so rough with Jordan was because they recognized his greatness. They knew that he was the greatest player in the world, and if they did not give him a setback by fouling him, trying to hurt him, or playing dirty, they had no chance of winning. Because he was the most gifted player on the court. It's funny, when we were kids playing football, everybody wanted the ball. We did not care that if we got the ball everybody was going to try to hit us, tackle us, throw us to the ground. We did not care that having the ball meant that it was almost certain that you would be thrown to the ground, which could be very painful. We did not care that if we got the ball, it was almost certain that we would be hit. How did we go from children who wanted the ball and did not care about getting hit or injured to adults in the game of life who are scared to get in the game because we fear opposition (getting hit)?

Speaking of sports, think of the greatest athletes you know. They refused to quit the game even when tragedy struck their lives and they experienced a setback. Michael Jordan's father was murdered at the height of his career; he experienced a setback. He retired for a year and a half, but he came back and won three more championships. Muhammad Ali's title was stripped, and he was banned from boxing in the prime of his career. He experienced a setback, but he came back and won the title three more times. Mike Tyson was sentenced to prison for three years during the prime of his career. He experienced a setback, but he came back and won the title when he was released. Allen Iverson was the number one high school basketball player in the nation and was sentenced to prison because he was supposedly involved in a brawl at a bowling alley. He experienced a setback, but he came back and went on to become the number one pick in the NBA draft. He also won NBA rookie of the year, the NBA MVP and became a hall of famer.

Magic Johnson was diagnosed with HIV; at that time, it was like a death sentence. He experienced a setback; he retired, and despite criticism and naysayers, he came back to the game. He won the MVP of the NBA all-star game the following year and won a gold medal with the dream team that summer after contracting HIV. In the next couple of years, he would coach the LA Lakers and then he would return as a player on the Lakers team in the 1995–1996 season. He also started a great business career, making more money in business than he did playing basketball.

Think if Magic was like most people when he heard one of the worst things a person could hear at that time, that they are HIV positive. He would have given up and died. He told the world that he would beat HIV. Most people thought that he would be dead within a year. Because of his faith, he let people know that having HIV was not a death sentence and you could live a productive life while having HIV.

Magic Johnson, as well as each of these athletes, had minor setbacks, but because of their faith and tenacity, they turned them into major comebacks. Because Magic was infected, it educated millions of heterosexuals and homosexuals about the disease and gave hope to people with the disease that if they took their medication, protected themselves, and stayed healthy, they could live a productive lifestyle and still make major contributions to society instead of being an outcast. This would not have happened if a high-profile person like Magic Johnson was not infected with the diseases or if Magic Johnson would have given up, given into self-pity, and died. We consider these athletes blessed and lucky to be famous millionaires, but that does not stop them from going through the storms of life and experiencing setbacks just like everybody else. My point is that the storms of life will come and tragic things will happen; we cannot deny that, and even when life is hard, we have to stay in the game in order to turn these setbacks into comebacks.

When I was going through my minor setback after the FBI had indicted me, and I was looking at ten years in prison for trumped-up charges of tax evasion, I knew the only reason I was going through these hard times was because of politics. I was a young African American politician who owned five businesses and was attempting to expand and own more, and I was also hands down the most effective and vocal politician in Winston-Salem, North Carolina. I was arguably the most vocal politician in the state of North Carolina. I was able to self-fund my campaign, so I never had to ask the powers-to-be for money. I had a saying: "I'm not here to raise money. I'm here to raise hell." While the other politicians were focused on social media, I was focused on social justice, fighting for the poor, and fighting for the underdog. I would often be quoted that I don't care about election day, I care about judgment day. I did not try to do what was popular; I tried my best to do what was right. I tried my best and was successful in improving the health outcomes of children in my county. I had another saying: "I'm not a politician who kisses babies, but I'm a politician who saves babies."

One day, somebody told me, "You have to make up your mind who you want to be. Do you want to be the black Warren Buffet or do you want to be the black Bernie Sanders? But you can't be both. You can be a quiet politician who will sell out and play the game and own a lot of businesses but you can't be a vocal politician speaking up for justice and own a lot of businesses." Sure enough, the FBI and IRS came after me for tax evasion. The prosecutor was a Republican who took down John Edwards in the middle of his presidential campaign, and he had a thing for going after Democrats. The FBI and IRS agents who were white Republicans claimed that I did not have the right to write off legitimate business expenses. They also claimed that I was under-reporting my income. Despite the appearance of hypocrisy, they went straight into the voting booth and voted for Trump, who had not paid a dime in taxes in ten of the last fifteen years, and one of those years, he only paid $500. If I was not doing something right by being a vocal politician or being an elected official in the first place, I would have never gone to prison. But at the end of the day, all of this was a minor setback for a major comeback. I would not choose what happened to me, but at the same time, I would not change what happened to me either. It made me better, not bitter. All that I went through was bad for the ego, but it was good for the soul.

CHAPTER 3:

LIFE IS A TEST

The next step to turning a minor setback into a major comeback is to realize that in life, you will be tested. To fulfil your calling, you must get in the game, but we all have to admit that the game of life can be tough. The game of life is full of tests. As a matter of fact, there is no learning without testing, and there is no promotion without testing. If you want to turn your minor setbacks into major comebacks, you must understand that in life, you will be tested before you will be promoted.

All that I went through, facing ten years in prison and eventually serving time in prison, losing my county commissioner seat, my good reputation being ruined, losing some of my businesses; I considered it a test of my faith. In school, you get the lesson, but then you get the test. The test reveals if you really learned the subject or not. The test reveals if you were paying attention or not. Can you apply what has been taught in class or not?

From all my reading, praying, studying, and meditating, God taught me patience. Now the test was here for me put into practice all that I had learned about patience. Through my reading, praying, studying, and meditating, God had taught me not to care about what people think. Now it was time to take the test to see if I could really apply what I had learned. From my reading, praying, studying, and meditating, I had learned to put my trust in God instead of in people or money. Now it was time to take the test to see if I really believed and could apply what I had been taught.

The teacher helps to instruct you during class, encourages you during class, and talks to you during class, but when you are taking the test, the teacher is silent. If you raise your hand when you are taking the test, the teacher will ignore you. If you raise your hand during class, the teacher will gladly answer your question, but during the time of testing, the teacher will pretend like he or she does not even see your hand. Sometimes during our toughest trials, it seems like God is silent or he is not talking to you or answering your prayers, but you have to remember the teacher is silent during the test and what you are going through is just a test.

That is the thing about faith. Faith that is not tested cannot be trusted. We don't need much faith when things are good. It's easy to work all day and night on your business when it makes a profit. What about when your business is losing money. When I first started my business the first year, I worked every day, and the business did not make a dime. The next year the business made over six hundred thousand. The next year the business broke the million-dollar mark, but it never would have happened if I was discouraged and refused to work when the business was not making any money. It's easy to have a good attitude when things are going your way. What about when things are bad?

In prison, I always had a smile on my face and a positive attitude. I was in prison, but the prison was not in me. In prison there where a lot of dope dealers, but I was a hope dealer. Some prisoners went to the dope dealer to get high and forget their problems, but I was a hope dealer. Prisoners were coming to me to get high and get over their problems. Some inmates chose to smuggle dope into the prison, but I chose to smuggle hope into the prison. I considered my time in prison as a test to see if I would be positive and hopeful during my incarceration. I considered it as a test to see if I would let my energy and faith change my circumstances or if I would let my circumstances change my energy and faith.

A test is not punishment. A test is given to evaluate where you are at. A test is given to see if you can advance to the next level of life. For a law student to become a lawyer, they must pass a test called the bar. To get your driver's license, you must take your driver's test. To become a doctor, you must take a test. To graduate, you have to take final exams. To get into law school, graduate school, medical school, or business school, you have to take the LSAT, GRE, MCAT, GMAT, etc. Setbacks are a form of testing and are not always bad. Tests and setbacks are an inevitable part of life for your promotion to come. Tests and setbacks let you know you are on the brink of going to the next level.

Some tests you can't even take unless you are qualified and ready. A student who has not graduated college cannot take the bar. A student must graduate college first, take the LSAT, pass the LSAT, graduate from law school, and then take the bar. The higher you go, the harder the tests. Certain tests and setbacks come in our lives to remind us how far we have come, and if we have passed previous tests and setbacks, we should have confidence that we will be able to pass this test or setback in front of us.

When David saw Goliath the giant (by the way, in life, we will be faced with giant tests), he did not complain to God and say, "Why is my life so hard? Why do I have to face this giant? Why is my life full of tests and setbacks?" He said, "I slayed the bear when I was tending sheep. I slayed the lion when I was tending sheep, and this philistine will be no different." A lot of us want the comeback, but we don't want the setback. We want the testimony, but we do not want the test. We want the message, but we don't want the mess. But guess what, there is no comeback without a setback. There is no testimony without a test, and there is no message without the mess. As a matter of fact, you can't even spell testimony without the word test, and you can't spell message without the word mess. David said, "I slayed the lion and the bear, and this philistine will be no different." When we have tests or setbacks, we need to look back on the previous tests we have passed; this will give us strength and courage, instead of complaining about how hard these tests are.

There is an old saying used by farmers and gardeners that says, "You can't pray for rain and complain about the mud." And so many times we pray to God for rain (blessings) but complain about the mud (tests). We also pray to be elevated but complain about the tests and setbacks in life, which are necessary for us to pass to go to the next level. When you look at gardening and planting seeds, you plant a seed in the ground, and that seed gives you a harvest of crops. You must cultivate the seed and guard it from worms and weeds. You must constantly water the crops, so they will grow and not become scorched by the sun. If the gardener really wants the plants to grow fast and grow strong, the gardener puts some fertilizer or manure on it. So, if you find yourself in deep sh%t and if you find yourself in the midst of a setback, don't worry, the master gardener is making sure you grow faster and stronger. As Nietzsche said, "What does not kill us makes us stronger."

In life there is a difference between being buried and being planted. When you are buried, you are put into the dirt where it is dark and it is over for you. When you are planted, you are put into the dirt where it is dark, but you are put there to grow and expand. You might be in a dark place and experiencing a setback right now, but you are not put into that dark place to die; you are put into that dark place to expand, grow, and comeback stronger than ever. There might be some manure in your life right now. You might be in a dark place right now. You might be in the middle of a setback right now. You might be in some deep sh@t right now, but that is nothing but fertilizer to help you grow stronger and comeback better than ever.

Remember when I asked you to eat the fruit and spit out the seeds? Well, this is the part of the book when you might want to do that. Think of Kim Kardashian, she is a perfect example of somebody who was in a dark place and experienced a setback, but she was not buried; she was planted. Instead of her career dying in the dirt and the darkness from a setback, her career grew and expanded in the dirt and the darkness. She was on a sex tape with the singer Ray J. That is very embarrassing, and that would have made most people go into hiding and ruin their life. Instead, she turned that tape into a reality show for her family. Then her sisters received their own reality show. They made hundreds of millions of dollars off the reality show. Because of the exposure to business opportunities, her little sister Kylie Jenner started her own makeup line. She is now the youngest self-made billionaire in America.

Her mother Chris Jenner is one of the most powerful business managers in the country. Kim is married to Kanye West, who is now a billionaire, and it is rumored that with her new cosmetics deal, she is a billionaire also. From a sex tape that seemed like it was a curse and a setback at the time, it turned out to be the biggest blessing in her life. They have made hundreds of millions from that sex tape, and they have two, possibly three, billionaires in their family. One being the youngest self-made billionaire in the country, and another, one of the richest rappers in the world.

You might say money is not everything, and you would be right, but quitting is everything, because if you quit, you would not get anything. If Kim Kardashian would have given up during her setback, become addicted to drugs, killed herself, or hid from the spotlight, this major comeback would have never happened, but instead of running from the spotlight and running from her problems, she took her newfound fame and capitalized off of it. Kim Kardashian suffered a minor setback, but because of her tenacity and persistence, she turned it into a major comeback.

I can hear some of you saying to me that the Kardashians are a terrible example. Well, let me give you another example. Look at Malcom X, his father was murdered by the KKK when he was young; that was a serious setback. His father was tied to railroad tracks and run over by a train. His father was a hardworking man and had a life insurance policy for his family, but his family could not collect it because the insurance company said his father committed suicide because his father was killed on the railroad tracks.

Without the money from his father's insurance policy, his family was pushed into deep poverty, another serious setback. His mother lost her mind and was put into an insane asylum, another serious setback. Malcom, his brothers, and his sisters were split up, another serious setback. He was sent to live with his older sister in Lansing Michigan. He eventually ended up serving a six-year prison sentence for crimes he would commit, another serious setback. In prison, he found religion through the Nation of Islam. In prison, it was rumored he read fifteen hours a day. When he came out of prison, his work ethic, knowledge, and compassion lead him to become the most famous minister in the Nation of Islam and one of the most effective advocates for the rights of black people during his time. He is recognized as one of the top black leaders of all time. The way he taught gave black people a sense of pride. Malcom made African Americans proud to be black. He made black people feel comfortable in their own skin. His autobiography is one of the greatest books ever written and has changed the way millions of people view racism.

He would not have had this compassion if he had not gone through all the struggles in his life. Malcom X suffered setbacks, but he turned them into comebacks. Because he had the setback of going to prison for six years and because, in prison, in the midst of his setback, he did not cry or complain but decided to read a book a day and gain the necessary knowledge, mindset, and articulation skills to impact a whole generation of African Americans who saw themselves as inferior under the ugly system of racism. A generation of people who felt they had to process their hair to make it straight like white people. Malcom X gave millions of black people a sense of pride and made millions of black people feel comfortable in their own skin. This would never have happened if he did not turn his minor setbacks into major comebacks.

CHAPTER 4:

GET RICH OR DIE TRYING

The next step in turning a minor setback into a major comeback is to be a hundred percent committed to your goals. When he crossed the Rubicon River, Julius Caesar knew that his army was outnumbered, and that the odds were against his army conquering Italy. Caesar knew that his soldiers knew those odds and it struck fear in them. Caesar decided to do something bold. In the middle of the night, when his soldiers were asleep, he ordered a few of his captains to burn the ships. When his soldiers saw the ships going up in flames, some of his soldiers were scared, some of them were angry, and some of them thought he was crazy.

Caesar told his army that the only way he or his troops would ever get back to see their wives, children, and homes was to defeat that huge army. They had only two options: win or die. With that resolve, knowing that there was no other way to see their children again, each man in Caesar's army fought like one hundred. The end of the story is that Caesar's army defeated the larger army and Caesar as well as his captains became legends.

When facing a setback, it is that burning of the ships mentality that it takes to achieve big dreams and turn your setbacks into comebacks. The rapper 50 Cent's first album was called *Get Rich or Die Trying*. DMX had the same attitude as Caesar, *Ride or Die*. What Caesar knew, what 50 Cent knew, and what DMX knew was this: In order to beat the odds, in order to survive setbacks and rise out of mediocrity and fulfill your dreams, you have to be all the way in, all the way invested, ten toes down. You can't do that with a plan B, looking back, because you won't fight with all of your strength if your life does not depend on winning the fight. Sometimes when you are all the way in, your faith will be tested, and you will experience dark times, but you have to remember it is always darkest before dawn.

Think about 50 Cent and his debut album, *Get Rich or Die Trying*. It was the highest-selling debut album in hip-hop history. I think all true fans of hip-hop will tell you that 50 Cent would not have sold those records if he had not suffered a setback by being shot nine times, which brought a lot of attention to 50 Cent. 50 cent is a genius marketer and a great businessman. He will tell you himself he is not the greatest lyricist, but he happened to turn tragedy into triumph and a setback into a comeback.

He was first signed to Columbia records. His record was going to be released, but it did not have much buzz. He released the single "How to Rob" that gave him a little attention but the album was not going to sell a million copies. It would probably not have gone gold.

Then something happened, a setback occurred in the form of him being shot nine times. Just like a setback hurts you at first, the shooting hurt 50 Cent at first. He was dropped from Columbia records, and his debut album never came out. It looked like the shooting was a curse, but it was really a blessing in disguise. As the saying goes, "Things don't happen to you, they happen for you." Because of the shooting, one of the bullets ended up going through 50 Cent's mouth. He was forced to go on a liquid diet. Which caused him to lose a lot of weight. Before, when 50 cent was on Columbia records, he was sort of chubby;

a major part of 50 Cent's appeal to women was that he was considered a sex symbol because he was in shape. Notice on the cover of *Get Rich or Die Trying*, he had his shirt off, showing his chiseled muscles; that was a major part of his image. He was the dark-skinned, thugged-out LL Cool J. He wrote a fitness book and was on the cover of many fitness magazines. He promoted and bought a stake in Vitamin Water, which was marketed as a health drink (even thought it was not healthy). When Pepsi Cola bought Vitamin Water, 50 Cent reportedly earned $150 million from the sale. None of this would have happened if 50 Cent would not have faced a setback by being shot and forced to go on a liquid diet, which caused him to lose the weight.

Since he faced the setback of being shot in his mouth, it caused his voice to change. He rapped with a slur that gave him a Southern-like drawl. At that time, Southern music was taking over hip-hop. Because of 50 Cent's voice, it made him appeal to a wider audience besides just the East Coast. This was important because East Coast hip-hop was declining at the time. Because he suffered the setback of being shot, he formed G-Unit for protection in the streets. He turned his G-Unit crew into a record label which is rumored that Interscope Records eventually gave 50 Cent $100 million for. This record label produced the careers of many artists and made several other millionaires. Because 50 Cent suffered the setback of being shot, it gave him street credibility. He seemed real when other rappers seemed fake.

This came at a time when a lot of fans were missing Tupac, and people were wondering who would be the next Tupac. Just like basketball fans wondered who would be the next Jordan. Fifty Cent surviving the setback of getting shot gave him that Tupac energy and aura, which attracted the attention of Eminem, Dr. Dre, and Interscope Records, Tupac's former record label. They put together a marketing campaign with 50 Cent with his shirt off, like Tupac. Fifty Cent was tattooed up, like Tupac. Fifty Cent was rapping about surviving, getting shot like Tupac. His first single was produced by Dr. Dre, like Tupac. He moved out to the West Coast, like Tupac. Fifty Cent had singles with Nate Dog and Snoop Dog, like Tupac. He dated Vivica, Fox like Tupac. He had a beef with Puffy, Nas, and Jay-Z, like Tupac. He went into acting, like Tupac. He even had a song with Tupac.

None of this would have happened if 50 Cent would not have been shot and decided that he was not going to quit just because he was facing adversity. After he was shot nine times, he faced another setback in the form of his record label dropping him, but he did not quit. His industry friends would not return his calls, but he did not quit. He risked his life to make music because the people who had him shot were involved in hip-hop, but he did not run and hide; he did not stop making music just because he was in the midst of a setback. He stuck to his calling and passion, even though by doing so, he was risking his life. He kept making music. As a matter of fact, he focused on his craft harder and made more music. A setback like a near-death experience would scare a lot of people, but it gave him focus and made him realize life is short and that he better take his craft seriously.

Because he would not give up, lie down, and die when he faced a minor setback, he was able to make a major comeback. Because he would not give up, *Get Rich or Die Trying* sold over twelve million copies. Because of this success, he was able to help a lot of people from his old neighborhood, give his friends record deals, help them sell millions of records, tour the world, and give them careers. He has the biggest show on television, *Power*. Power has elevated Courtney Kemp, a black woman to one of the most powerful women in Hollywood. The show also birthed the career of Omar Warrick and Joseph Sikora.

Power took them and so many others to the next level. He has other TV shows coming out. He is creating new stars and helping other people's dreams comes true; this would not have happened if he did not face the setback of getting shot.

One of the reasons they call Muhammad Ali the greatest is not because of his boxing record. Muhammad Ali lost some fights, and there are other boxers who are undefeated or loss less fights. Ali is not considered the greatest because of his charisma, showmanship, or athletic ability; not even because he was outspoken for justice and spoke out against the Vietnam War; not because he sacrificed the prime of his career for refusing to sign up for the draft. All of these events played a part in the reason so many people call Ali the greatest till this day. However, the main reason people call Ali the greatest is because he was never knocked out. He was knocked down plenty of times, but he always got up. He was knocked down, but he was never knocked out; every time he was knocked down, he got up.

If you want to be great, every time you face a setback and you are knocked down, get up. There has never been a boxer that has not been knocked down, but Ali was one of those rare boxers who got up every time he was knocked down. Life will give you setbacks and knock you down, but you have to get up. Never quit. The Bible says that a righteous man falls seven times but yet rises, but the wicked falls when calamity strikes. Even righteous people fall and face setbacks, but what makes them righteous is that they get up.

Eric Thomas said that people can call you anything, but make sure they don't call you a quitter. It's not good to lie, but there are financially successful and rich liars, but there are no successful and rich quitters. People can call you crooked; it's not good to be crooked, but there are rich crooks, but there are not any rich or financially successful quitters (unless they inherited their money or won the lottery). Quitters never fulfill their dreams.

Persistent people begin where most people quit. Muhammad Ali says that the fight does not start until he gets hit. Most people quit in life when they get hit one good time or face a setback. Ali said the fight did not start until he got hit. NBA players have a saying during the playoffs that the series does not start until the home team loses on their court. Notice that the home team is the favorite to win and should win. Most people quit when they face a setback by losing when they are supposed to win. When they planned to win, prepared to win, and they don't win, it can crush their confidence more than attempting something that is against the odds. Because in the back of a person's mind, when they are attempting something that is against the odds, they did not think they would succeed anyway. But professional athletes say the series does not start till somebody loses a game when they are supposed to win.

That's the difference between winners and losers. Winners put everything in perspective. They have self-discipline and do not get too high when things are good or too low when things are bad. Winners display commitment. As the saying goes, one person with commitment, persistence, and endurance will accomplish more than a thousand people with interest alone. If you want to turn your minor setbacks into major comebacks, you have to know that persistence overcomes resistance. You have to make a quality decision that you will fulfill your dreams and your goals. You have to refuse to turn back, and if you keep marching toward your destination, you will turn your setbacks into comebacks in due time.

CHAPTER 5:

VICTORY

The next step in order to turn a minor setback into a major come-back is to never give up. In life, we are called to be winners, we are called to be triumphed. We are called to turn our setbacks into comebacks. Life is like a game, a battle, a sport, or a war. In a game, there are four quarters. You can lose a quarter; it does not mean you have lost the game. You can lose the first three quarters and still win the game if you win the fourth quarter by the right margin. In sports, there are playoff series, and in that series, there might be seven games. You can lose a game and win the series. You can lose three games and still win the series if you win four games.

The same rules apply with war; you can lose some battles and still win the war. Don't give up because you have faced some setbacks. Don't give up because you have lost some quarters. Don't give up because you have lost some games. Don't give up because you have lost some bat-tles. You can still win the war or the series if you do not give up. Don't give up because you have lost some rounds; you can still win the fight.

Why is Jordan considered by many to be the greatest basketball player ever? It is not because of the six championships he won; Bill Russell has won eleven championships, and Kareem has won six cham-pionships also. Kareem has more MVPs than Jordan and has scored more points than Jordan. Jordan is considered the greatest for many reasons, but one of the main reasons we consider him the greatest is because he is the most clutch player ever to play the game. His team can be losing, and Jordan will hit the last-second shot to win the game. We remember Jordan beating the Utah Jazz with the last-second shot. We remember him beating Cleveland with the last-second shot. We don't remember the easy games Jordan played in; that is not what made him great. What made Jordan great is that in the games they were losing and facing a setback, he would not quit. He willed his team to a comeback, and he hit the last-second shot.

That's what we love about Jordan; he refused to give up when things got hard. When he was facing a setback, he played to the last second and he hit the game winner. He made sure his team came back. What if Jordan was like most people and started to complain, cry, and ask God why when it looked like his team was losing. What if Jordan's team was down by ten points in the fourth quarter, and he walked off the floor and quit. We would look at him like he was crazy, but this is how we treat our life when we are down by ten in the fourth quarter. We are facing a setback and we quit; no wonder we don't fulfill our destinies.

Think about LeBron James. What is his biggest win? It is coming back to Cleveland and beating the Golden State Warriors team that had won seventy-three games. This was a team that had the best record in NBA history, better than Michael Jordan's Chicago Bulls team that won seventy-two games. Steph Curry was the first and only unanimous NBA MVP. Cleveland was down three to one. No team in NBA history has ever come back from three games down in the NBA finals to win the NBA championship. It seemed like it was impossible for Cleveland to win. All the experts wrote LeBron James off.

Then something special happened in game five, LeBron James had over forty points. In game six, LeBron had over forty points again. In game seven, LeBron had a triple-double, leading his team to the biggest finals comeback in NBA history. LeBron is considered one of the greatest by many because of that victory. All because he was the underdog, and it looked like there was no chance of him coming from behind, but he did it, and the city of Cleveland, the city where people who once burned his jerseys in the street, loved him more than ever.

People love the underdog. Where do you think we get that from? We probably get it instinctively from God. David was the biggest underdog when he slayed Goliath, and God called David a man after his own heart. God told Moses to go against Pharaoh, the most powerful man on earth with the most powerful army. Gold told the children of Israel to kill the giants. God always wants you to defy the odds. When God is on your side, you will be the underdog. Because if you had the most money, if you had the biggest army, if you had the most backers, God would not get the glory. Anybody can win with the odds in their favor, but when you win against overwhelming odds, people know that God is with you. The odds might be overwhelming for you to become a millionaire, but you can reach that goal. The odds might be overwhelming for you to finish your PhD, but you can do it. The odds might be overwhelming for you to be the first person in your family to finish college, but you can do it. The odds might be overwhelming for you to start that business, but you can do it.

It might seem like nobody is in your corner, but remember God plus one is a majority. If God be for you, who can be against you? You can't win a fight if you are not in the fight. In life, there is always going to be a fight; there is always going to be a challenge; there is always going to be a setback, but we are called to win; we are called to turn our setbacks into comebacks.

You cannot win a game if you are not in the game. Champions are people who have been through fights and come out victorious. You are not a champion if you have been involved in only one fight and won. In boxing, it usually takes about twenty or thirty fights to get a shot at the champion. Life is a fight, so let's not be scared when it seems like we are in a fight; that is how life is designed.

Most of us have heard of Norman Vincent Peale, the author of *The Power of Positive Thinking*, which has sold over twenty million copies and is one of the bestselling self-help books of all time. What most people don't know is the fact that *The Power of Positive Thinking* was almost never published. Peale was in his fifties when he wrote the book, and he received nothing but a stack of rejection slips. He faced a setback.

Feeling rejected, he threw the manuscript of the book into a trash can and told his wife not to remove it. She took him literally, and the next day, she took the trash can with the manuscript in it to a publisher and got a book deal. If his wife would not have persisted when Peale gave up, he would not have become the founder of the human potential movement. The whole self-help industry as we know it would have been different or would not exist as we know it today because that book has influenced so many people and so many self-help authors. The lesson in Peale's story is that everybody gets discouraged. Everybody faces a setback, even the person who wrote *The Power of Positive Thinking*. The founder of the human potential movement even gave into discouragement, but we have to persist despite our discouragement.

The Bible says that he who puts his hands to the plow and looks back is not fit for the kingdom of God. The reason it says this is because plowing is like chasing your dream; it is hard work, and you are always tempted to quit. You have to be persistent; a lot of things are God's will for you to have, but if you give up, you will not obtain them. God told Moses to go to Pharaoh and tell him to "Let my people go." It was clearly God's will for the children of Israel to be delivered from slavery in Egypt, but it would not have happened if Moses was not persistent. When Moses went to Pharaoh and said, "Let my people go," Pharaoh did not say okay and let the people go. Moses had to keep coming back to Pharaoh; each time he came back, he came back harder.

Moses invented the term escalation. If Moses was like most people today, he would have given up the first time Pharaoh said no. He would have rationalized it in his mind and said "maybe it was not God's will to let the people go." "If it was God's will to let the people go, why did Pharaoh say no?" "If God really wanted his people to be let free, he would have made Pharaoh say yes." "Maybe I did not really see that burning bush, I was probably just dreaming."

"I should have stayed in Egypt where life was easy, and I was Pharaoh's grandson." "Why did I save that Hebrew slave from being beaten by the Egyptian?" "I gave up the good life." I had it made living in the palace." If Moses was like most people, all these thoughts would have made him quit when things did not work out as soon as he wanted them too.

Just like Moses gave up the comfort and prestige of living in the palace in Egypt and the title of being the grandson of Pharaoh, you might have given up a stable career and cashed in on your 401k and retirement to start a business, and you might feel like Moses in that it is not working as fast as you want it. Like Moses, don't give up, stay with it, and it will work out. You might have had a good job in Corporate America. But you felt led to open up your own business, and it is not quite growing as fast as you want. Instead of making six figures like you were in corporate America, now you are losing money. Like Moses, stick with it, and it will turn around.

When asked about who was the greatest president of all times in a poll, most Americans named Abraham Lincoln. But his rise to fame was not glamorous at all. He suffered more setbacks than any other president in the history of the United States. He dropped out of grade school, ran a business, and went broke. Because of that setback, it took him fifteen years to pay off his bills.

His wife that he loved dearly died and as a result he suffered a nervous breakdown. He had four sons but only one lived long enough to become an adult. He ran for the House of Representatives and lost twice. He ran for the senate and lost twice. He delivered a speech that would become a classic, but when he gave it, the audience did not like it. He was attacked by the press daily and despised by half the country. Some people will say that despite these setbacks, he become the greatest president of all time, but I will say that it is because of these setbacks that he became the greatest president of all time.

Because he dropped out of school, was a failure in business, and lost four elections before becoming president, he had the understanding, experience, and emotional maturity to come back from a loss. So, during the Civil War when the Northern Army lost to the Confederate Army at battle run, he could stay poised and calm because he was familiar with the emotions that come with defeat and setbacks. Everybody was urging Lincoln to negotiate for peace after that loss, but because of his experience with failure and setbacks, he knew how fortunes could turn in one's favor if that person, army, or country did not give up.

He was continually criticized during the war because the North did not have a decisive victory until Ulysses S Grant finished off the siege at Vicksburg in 1863, followed soon by the Northern victory at Gettysburg. People held Lincoln as a genius and a hero for the moment, but it did not go to his head. Because Lincoln had won elections and lost elections. Because Lincoln had been popular and unpopular. Because Lincoln had faced setbacks and turned them into comebacks. He had developed the emotional strength to not let the praise of the people go to his head nor let the criticism of the people and media get to his heart. He stayed steady and focused, realizing the war was far from over.

Six months later, the Northern armies led by General Grant got bogged down trying to chase General Robert E. Lee and the Confederate Army. Casualties mounted, the death tolls of Northern troops, and Confederate troops kept rising. He started receiving criticism again from his generals. The public and the media urged him to negotiate with the South for terms of peace.

Lincoln become very unpopular with the American people. They believed the war was taking too long and too many Americans had died. According to polls, most Americans believed Lincoln should negotiate for peace. In August of 1864, feeling the weight of all this pressure, Lincoln drafted a letter, spelling out the terms of peace he would offer the South. But the same night, he felt ashamed of himself for losing his resolve and hid the letter in his drawer. A week later, the tide turned, and the North put together a string of victories that would crush the Confederate Army for good. If Lincoln had not gone through the horrific setbacks of having the wife, he loved die and having buried three of his four sons, if he was not familiar with the emotions and pain of death personally, he would have probably folded and negotiated for peace when the death tolls in the civil war started to rise.

During the civil war, it is estimated that anywhere between 620,000 to 1.2 million Americans died in the war. It is a war that has had more American casualties than all other wars that America participated in combined. If Lincoln would have folded and negotiated with the South for peace, slavery would not have ended then and who knows how long it would have been before slavery was abolished. It could have been fifty to one hundred years from that date. If he would have negotiated for peace, all of those American casualties would have been in vain.

A leader or another American president that did not have the horrific experiences of facing setbacks like losing the woman he loved or burying three sons and coming back from it, dropping out of school, losing four elections, and going broke in business would not have had the emotional maturity and courage to stick with the war until the South folded. A person with an easier path to the White House probably would have given up after the North lost those early victories to the South and would have struck a compromise that would have allowed slavery to continue to exist. When Lincoln's wife died, it seemed like a curse. When three of his four sons died it seemed like a curse. When he lost those elections, it seemed like a curse, when he went bankrupt in business, it seemed like a curse, but it was really a blessing to this nation and this world. Because he would not give up, he was able to turn those minor setbacks into major comebacks.

CHAPTER 6:

LIFE OF A HERO

The next step in turning your minor setback into a major comeback is to identify with your inner hero. You have to see yourself as a hero because we are all heroes to somebody. As little kids, all of us wanted to be heroes, whether it is was Superman, Batman, Wonder Woman, Captain America, Black Panther, The Hulk, Iron Man, Spider Man, etc. In these comic books and cartoons, these heroes went through hell. They faced serious setbacks, and they were beaten half to death. Some of them died and came back; they were captured, they were knocked unconscious, and they lost their powers.

Batman's mother and father were killed. Superman's parents were killed and his planet destroyed. Spider man's uncle that raised him was murdered. Black Panther's father was murdered. Iron Man's father was murdered. These heroes faced setbacks, went through hell, and it seemed like every week, when a new issue of the comic book or cartoon came out, they suffered more setbacks and went through more hell, but at the end of the day they saved the world every week and defeated the evil villain every week.

These hard times and setbacks are what made these super heroes want to use their powers for good. Superman would not have tried so hard to save the planet Earth if he did not suffer setbacks. He was fueled by the pain of his mother and father dying and the planet that he came from, Krypton, being destroyed. Because of the pain that resulted from the setback of his planet being destroyed, it fueled him to save the planet Earth. Bruce Wayne would probably have been another spoiled rich kid if he did not suffer the horrific setback of seeing his parents killed in front of his face, and he was so young that he was powerless to do anything about it. The pain of that setback fueled him to train to become the best martial artist and become the vigilante known as the Batman. The pain of the setback of not being able to save his parents fueled him to become the best vigilante and to stop street crime in Gotham City. And since he could not save his parents, he vowed he would try his best to save the world.

In all of these cases, the superheroes were faced with setbacks, but because they refused to quit, they refused to fold, they used the pain of those unfortunate events to turn those setbacks into comebacks. Because they went through the pain of the setback and survived it, they were able to help others who were going through the pain or stop others from going through the pain.

As we grow older, we start to admire different heroes who saved the world or this nation. MLK, JFK, Abraham Lincoln, and Bobby Kennedy; we all know what happened to them. It's amazing as kids we want to be like heroes but when we grow older, we decide all that drama is not worth it, and there is a part of me that understands totally. As matter of fact, I don't understand it; I over stand it. So, we grow up and we decide to stay in our comfort zone; we are almost like the turtle in the shell. When a turtle is in its shell, it is immune to danger for the most part, but it cannot travel anywhere unless it comes out of its shell. We play it safe, and we lose hope, joy, and enthusiasm.

Think of Martin Luther King Jr. A man who in his own auto-biography said he grew up living a privileged life. King grew up in a prominent family in Atlanta, Georgia, where he was taught that it was a blessing to be black. In Atlanta, there where examples of successful black businesspeople, preachers, and professionals. Even during periods of segregation in the country, there were very successful black people in Atlanta who were like black royalty. His father, Martin Luther King Sr., was a very prominent preacher. He had a very strong relationship with Benjamin Mays who is arguably the greatest black educator of all time. Not to mention one of the greatest African Americans to live during his generation.

Martin Luther King Jr. was surrounded by African Americans who gave him a sense of pride and self-worth even during the period of segregation (self-worth and pride that would be severely tested in the coming years). Martin Luther king Jr. was accepted to Morehouse at the age of fifteen. He would then attend Crozier Theological Seminary and University of Boston School of Theology, one of the best theology schools in the country. Martin Luther king Jr. met his wife, Coretta, in Boston. He was a young African American preacher with a PhD in Boston. He was in high demand. Coretta wanted him to take one of the jobs offered to him to become a professor at one of the many universities in Boston. His father wanted him to come back to Atlanta. His father had a job as a professor lined up for young Martin at Morehouse. His father was also willing to make him associate pastor at Ebenezer Baptist Church and prepare him to take over the church.

Martin Luther King Jr.'s instincts led him to go to Montgomery, Alabama. When he told Coretta, she disagreed. Coretta was from Alabama, and she knew how racist Alabama was. She knew, in Alabama, there was no Atlanta with prominent blacks to shield Martin and herself from racism. She wanted King to stay up North. His father thought he was crazy; he knew how racist whites were in Alabama and reminded the young King that he had lived a sheltered life that protected him from the racism that the average African American has experienced. First as a prominent member of Atlanta society and second as a student in liberal Boston, and although Atlanta and Boston had their own problems with racism, they were nothing like Alabama.

Although King valued the advice of his beloved wife and father, he could not be persuaded. King believed that being the pastor of Dexter Avenue Baptist Church was the right move. So, King, his wife, Coretta, and their young daughter moved to Montgomery. If King would have never followed his heart and moved to Montgomery, the world would probably never have known him as the Martin Luther King Jr. we know today. If he would have chosen the life of comfort and chosen to stay in Boston or move back to Atlanta, we would certainly not be celebrating his birthday as a national holiday.

When King arrived in Montgomery, residents asked him to become president of the local NAACP. He declined the offer, choosing to focus on pastoring at Dexter Baptist Church, which he loved dearly, and focused on raising his family. The Montgomery bus boycott started when Rosa Parks refused to give her seat to a white man. The bus boycott started to gain momentum, and local leaders asked Martin Luther King Jr. to lead the boycott. Just like the offer to lead the local NAACP, he again refused. Eventually, the bus boycott gained so much momentum that they had to create a separate organization outside of the NAACP to lead the boycott. The MIA was created.

Local leaders came to King, asking him to lead this organization, expecting him to say no, but to their delight, he accepted the invitation. Within weeks of accepting the position of the MIA, he started receiving multiple death threats every day. Notice that when you find your true calling and start on your road to your destiny, the setbacks start to occur. Martin Luther King Jr. never received any death threats when he was content to preach and serve his small congregation. If he would have stayed content to just be a preacher and never gotten involved in the bus boycott, he probably would never have received any death threats. He might still be alive today, but society would be worse off and he would have never fulfilled his calling.

As soon as he took over the MIA, he was arrested for tax evasion. Local police used local African American preachers to use a whispering campaign against him that turned some African Americans against him. Part of the whisper campaign was a rumor that he stole MIA money and bought himself a new Cadillac and his wife a new Buick. He was arrested for speeding and thrown in a jail cell with the most hardened criminals. He posted bail, and the trial was set for two days later with a bunch of trumped-up charges. The night before his trial he received a phone call. "Nigger, we tired of your mess now. And if you ain't out of town in three days, we going to blow your brains out and blow up your house." Something in the tone of the caller's voice sent chills down King's spine. To King, it seemed like more than just a threat.

In the midst of his setback, King tried to sleep that night, but he couldn't, the man's voice was constantly replaying in his mind. He went into his kitchen to make coffee and calm himself down. He was shaking. He was losing his nerve and his confidence. He thought about a way to bow out of the leadership of the MIA and return to the comfortable life of just being a minster. As he examined himself and contemplated his past, he realized that up until these weeks, he had never had a setback and he had never faced real adversity. His life had been relatively easy, happy, and free of setbacks. His parents had given him everything. He had not known what it was like to go through a setback and feel such intense anxiety.

As he went deeper with these thoughts, he realized that he had simply inherited religion from his father. He had never personally communicated with God or felt his presence. He thought of his daughter and his wife that he loved. He couldn't take much more of this. He could not call his father for advice or solace; it was well past midnight. He felt a wave of panic.

Suddenly, it came to him, there was only one way out of this crisis. He bowed over his cup of coffee and prayed with an urgency he had never felt before. "Lord, I must confess that I'm weak now. I'm faltering. I'm losing my courage. And I can't let the people see me like this. Because if they see me weak and losing my courage, they will begin to get weak. At that moment, clear as could be, he heard a voice from within: "Martin Luther, stand up for righteousness, stand up for justice, stand up for truth and lo I will be with you even until the end of the world." The voice, that of the Lord, promised to never leave him, to come back to him when he needed it. Almost immediately, he felt a sense of tremendous relief. The burden of his doubts and anxiety had lifted from his shoulders. He could not help but cry.

Several nights later, when King was attending an MIA meeting, he faced a serious setback in the form of his house being bombed. It was a blessing his wife and daughter were unharmed. When informed of the setback, he remained calm. Black supporters rallied around his house, advocating revenge and violence for the bombing. He informed the crowd that he attended to stay nonviolent. I can only imagine how hard it was for King to stick to nonviolence after his house was bombed with his wife and daughter in it. I'm sure everything in his being wanted to pick up a gun and kill a racist person, but he stuck to his principles.

After the bombing, his father pleaded with him to return to Atlanta, but he decided to stay. Coretta's father drove to town to take her back home and away from King, but she could not leave the man she loved. King and Coretta decided that their daughter should go and stay with Coretta's parents. Ninety-Nine percent of black leaders or white leaders today would have left town and quit if they faced a setback like their house being bombed. Trust me, I have been in politics for years; 99.999 percent of black leaders or white leaders would have left town and never would have come back, no pun intended. As a matter fact, being in politics, I know a lot of preachers and political leaders. You don't have to threaten their lives; all you have to do is threaten to cancel a check and that is enough to make them quit, but King was different.

I'm sure in the back of his mind, in the midst of these setbacks, he constantly thought about why he gave up the opportunity to live the good life by being a professor in Boston or at Morehouse. But instead, he followed his heart, and following his heart had him on the verge of losing his family and his life. The blessing in all these setbacks and tragedies was that because of the stress and strain of being arrested on trumped-up tax charges and daily death threats, he developed a relationship with God. Because his house was bombed with his wife and daughter in it, he had personally experienced racism first hand. This experience put a hunger in him to end racism.

With his newfound relationship with God and his hunger to end racism that was born from the traumatic setback of his house being bombed, it propelled King to work tirelessly and fear nothing or nobody. Because of these setbacks, he developed an ultimate trust in God. As a matter fact, he was quoted as saying, "I would rather be dead than scared." Since he experienced these setbacks, his only goal was to end racism and make the lives of African Americans and all Americans better.

If King would not have personally been through these setbacks, he would not have had the strength to lead the people to fight against Bull Connor. If his house would not have been bombed or if he decided to act in a violent way instead of a nonviolent way to the bombing, he would not have had the moral authority to tell thousands of marchers to remain nonviolent even when they were sprayed with water hoses, beaten by cops, or bitten by dogs. He could tell marchers to be restrained because he himself was restrained. If he had not developed that relationship with God, he could not have survived the constant attacks, probes, investigations by the FBI (take it from me, the FBI is the most powerful foe and the most racist foe a person can face. You don't know racism or power until you have had a fight with the FBI).

If he had not have faced the setback of his house being bombed and he did not have that relationship with God, he might have folded every time he was arrested, but he used his periods of incarceration to write like the Apostle Paul. His most famous letter being the letter from Birmingham Jail. If he had not had that relationship with God, he would have folded in negotiations with President Kennedy and President Johnson. He would have ended up going to the white house, coming back to the black community, and articulating President Johnson's agenda. But instead, because of his courage and relationship with God, he went to the White House and articulated black people's agenda to President Johnson.

Because of the setbacks he experienced in Montgomery, it shaped him into the leader that could lead the charge for the passage of the Civil Rights Act, Voting Rights Act, Great Society Programs, War on

Poverty, March on Washington, Poor People's Movement, and become one of the most vocal critics of the Vietnam War.

If he would not have received all those death threats, if he would not have been arrested on trumped-up tax charges in Montgomery, if his house was not bombed with his wife and daughter in it, one can strongly infer that Martin Luther King Jr. would not have had the strength to be the greatest leader of our time. We have a long way to go, but we would not be as far as we are today without King and thousands of other who sacrificed to fight racism. Just like King, when you are facing a setback, you need to pray more. You need to read more. You need to draw closer to God. This will give you the spiritual, emotional, and mental strength to turn your minor setbacks into major comebacks.

CHAPTER 7:

LIFE IS A FIGHT

Another key to turning your minor setback into a major comeback is to fight for your dreams. At the time when I was elected county commissioner, I was the youngest African American ever to be elected county commissioner in an urban county in North Carolina. I had a lot of political influences and a lot of personal influences in my life that motivated me. But I would say the two people who influenced me the most that I did not know personally were Barack Obama and the fictional character Rocky. For obvious reasons, Barack Obama being the first African American president in the history of this country influenced me greatly. After the election of Barack Obama, a whole wave of younger people started winning elections based on the change message and that wave is still happening till this day. But the story of Obama's rise was not so glamorous according to his wife Michelle Obama.

Barack was the first African American ever to be elected president of the *Harvard Law Review*. He could have accepted a job offer anywhere. There were so many corporate law firms willing to offer him six-figure salaries, but he would not take those offerings. He could have easily taken a job at any of these corporate law firms and quickly become a millionaire with no problem. Instead, he decided to enter politics and teach constitutional law at the University of Chicago. He eventually became state senator. Spending his time as a state senator and teaching constitution law classes did not make Obama a lot of money, considering the fact that he had two young daughters and a six-figure student loan debt.

Michelle Obama had a great job. She was the bread winner in the family, and Barack pursed his dream and calling as a politician. Barack always had ambition for a higher office. When Barack hinted that he believed that he could be president of the USA, Michelle laughed at him and stated that she did not believe that any black person could be president of the United States of America. She loved Barack and her family, and she constantly tried to get him to quit politics because politics can be so vicious and corrupt. And plus, they had a new family, and she felt that Barack should get a great-paying job to provide a great life for their daughters. Barack eventually ran for higher office when he ran for Congress and lost to the former Black Panther Bobby Rush. Bobby Rush received 61 percent of the vote, and Barack only received 31 percent of the vote. Receiving a political beating that bad destroys most young politicians' careers. This type of loss would have discouraged most people from staying in politics, and it probably discouraged Barack, but he did not quit like most people would have. Instead, because Barack loved politics and was persistent, he turned that minor setback into a major comeback.

He served in the state senate for several more years when finally, a US Senate seat opened up. He told his wife that this was his last shot to follow his dream of being a big-time politician and that if this did not work out, he would get a job paying good money. When he ran for US Senate in the Democratic Party, he was down in the polls. His competitors were raising more money than him. But he did not allow these setbacks to stop him from making a comeback.

Barack ended up winning the Democratic primary. He was picked as a keynote speaker at the 2004 Democratic National Convention and instantly became a superstar and the hottest name in politics and soared to a landslide victory over Allen Keys. Four years later, after victories over Hillary Clinton and John McCain, he become president of the United States. This would have never happened if Barack would have allowed his setbacks to make him quit on his dreams or if he would have put money over his passion.

My second inspiration was *Rocky*. For two reasons. First, I was the underdog and going against probably the most well-known politician in my city when I ran for County Commissioner. The campaign was just like Rocky fighting Apollo Creed. Second, the theme music to *Rocky* inspired me to exercise and lose weight in order to get in shape for the campaign. I worked out to the theme music of *Rocky* every day. Also, the theme music gave me motivation to knock on doors for six hours every day for six months in order to win the election.

All of us have heard of *Rocky*, but few of us have heard the story about how *Rocky* was created. According to Tony Robinson, Sylvester Stallone believed from a young age he was meant to be a star. The problem was, agents could not stand his voice and they did not think that he was a star. He kept getting rejected. He kept facing setbacks. He said he got kicked out of 1500 agents' offices in New York. Stallone was telling this story to a friend and the friend replied that there are not 1500 agents in New York. Stallone said yeah, I know, I was kicked out some of those agents' offices five, six, seven, eight, nine times.

Stallone remembers one particular agent. He arrived at the agent's office at four o'clock in the afternoon, and the agent would not see him. Stallone did not go home; instead, he spent the night in the lobby of the agent's office until he could see the agent the next morning. That's how Sylvester Stallone finally got his first role in a movie. It was a movie nobody had ever heard of; he played a thug in the movie and got killed off in twenty seconds. He did three movies like that where he got killed off instantly and was only on screen for about twenty seconds.

He kept trying to get better roles, but he kept getting rejection after rejection. He kept facing setbacks. So, he changed his approach. Stallone was starving and could not even afford to have heat in his apartment. His wife was furious at him; they use to fuss and fight all the time. She would tell him he just needed to get a job. His friend asked him in the interview about why he did not just take his wife's advice and get a job. Stallone said that he did not get a job because if he got a job and paid his bills, he would lose his hunger and the desire to fulfill his goal. Stallone said he needed all that pain and he needed to burn all his bridges in order to fulfill that goal. Stallone said that if he got a job, he believed he would be seduced into a comfortable lifestyle and he would lose his dream. He said he had to keep his hunger and his hunger was his only advantage.

Stallone's wife did not understand that at all, and they always had these vicious fights and arguments. It was the middle of the winter; it was freezing, and they had no heat. Stallone used to go to the library because it was warm. Stallone had never read anything before, but when he went to the library, he started to read the poems of Allen Edger Poe, because somebody left that book at the table he was sitting at. Reading Poe got him to stop thinking about himself and start to think about how he could help others. Reading Poe was what made him decide to become a writer.

Stallone tried to write a bunch of screenplays but nothing worked. He was so broke that he did not even have fifty dollars. He finally sold a script called Paradise Alley, and he sold it for a hundred dollars. He was excited when he sold the script, but it never led to anything. He kept trying to break in the business, but it never happened. He kept facing setbacks. He was so broke that he sold his wife's jewelry (which was a big mistake); after that, she hated him and she left him. He had no money or food. He said the only thing that he had is what he loved the most, his dog.

He loved his dog because his dog gave him unconditional love. He was so broke that he could not even afford to feed his dog. He went to the liquor store, which was the lowest day of his life, and he stood outside the liquor store, trying to sell his dog for fifty dollars. Finally, somebody actually agreed to buy his dog but only for twenty-five dollars. Sylvester Stallone admits it was the lowest and worst day of his life.

Two weeks later, he was watching Muhammad Ali fight Chuck Wepner, a white guy that nobody thought had a shot of lasting three rounds with Ali. No matter how much Muhammad Ali hit and beat Chuck Wepner, he would not go down. Chuck Wepner went the distance, and Muhammad Ali won by a decision, but he did not knock Chuck Wepner out. Sylvester Stallone was so inspired by this fight that he came up with the script for *Rocky*. He wrote *Rocky* that night; he spent twenty straight hours writing *Rocky*. He did not even go to sleep. He tried to sell the script of *Rocky*, but he was constantly turned down by agents and executives. He kept facing setbacks.

He finally received an offer to sell the script of *Rocky* for $125,000. That was a lot of money back then and more money than Sylvester Stallone had ever seen in his life. He told the agents that he wanted to star in the movie *Rocky* and play the lead role. They said that they would buy the script, but they did not believe in his acting ability, they did not want him in the movie nevertheless the lead role. How many of us would have taken the money? Stallone did not; he said that Rocky was him and that if he could not play the lead role, he would not sell the script.

The studio turned him down and did not buy the script for $125,000. Stallone was still broke. After a couple weeks, the studio called him again and doubled the amount of money to $250,000 to buy the script but still did not offer him the lead role. How many of us would have taken that quarter of a million dollars? Stallone did not take the money, and he was still broke. Finally, the studio agreed to give him the lead role, but they only offered him $35,000 and points on the movie because they did not believe in him as an actor.

They told Stallone that they were not willing to put a lot of money behind an unproven actor in the lead role. When Stallone received the $35,000, he went back to the liquor store day after day to find the man he sold his dog to. He finally saw the man and told the man his story and that he would like to buy the dog back. The man said, "No way, I love this dog." Stallone said, "You bought the dog from me for twenty-five dollars. I am willing to buy it back from you for a hundred dollars." The man said no. Stallone then said $500; the man said no. Stallone said $1,000; the man said no. Stallone finally ended up buying the dog back at $15,000, and he gave the man a role in *Rocky*. It is the same dog that was in *Rocky*, which was one of the most emotional parts of the movie.

Long story short, it only took $1 million to make *Rocky*, but *Rocky* grossed over $200 hundred million. *Rocky* has inspired millions of people and is one of the most inspirational movies of all time. And there are over eight movies in the *Rocky* series. The majority of people who do not know the Stallone story would say he is lucky, but that's not the case. Stallone knew what he wanted and made up his mind to get it.

In the process of making *Rocky*, Stallone faced some minor setbacks, but he turned them into a major comebacks.

Think if Sylvester Stallone would have landed his first job without going through the struggle, without going through the setback of rejection. One can make the assumption that he never would have become a script writer. One can assume that there never would have been a *Rocky* series or a *Rambo* series, two of the most successful movie series of all time. *Rocky* is definitely the most inspiring movie and inspiring movie series of all time. The reason there is a *Rocky* is because Stallone felt like he was the underdog, because he was turned down for so many roles. If he did not have these heartbreaking experiences, there most likely would not have been a *Rocky* movie or *Rocky* series.

Stallone getting turned down for roles seemed like a curse, but it was really a blessing. He faced so many setbacks in starting his acting and writing career, but he turned those setbacks into comebacks. Because he was turned down, was the underdog, experienced so many setbacks, he was able to write the ultimate underdog movie that has inspired millions.

That's why Stallone makes inspirational movies like *Rocky* where the underdog eventually defies the odds and wins. If you notice in all of the *Rocky* series movies, the star of the movie, whether it be Rocky or Creed, always loses the first fight. The star always has a setback, but guess what, in the end, the star always comes back. Just because you lose the first fight, don't quit. You notice in the *Rocky* series, Rocky lost his first title shot and Creed's son lost his first title shot, but they did not give up. Think about his movies in the *Rambo* series; it's a sole soldier against a whole army, and that soldier wins even though the odds are against him.

Sometimes when you are trying to achieve your goals, destiny, or dreams, it feels like the whole world is against you. The moral of the *Rocky* and *Rambo* stories is, even though it seems like the whole world is against you, you can still win the battles, wars, and fights that are raging against you and fulfill your dreams. The moral of the *Rocky* and *Rambo* stories is that even though you face a minor setback, you can turn it into a major comeback if you do not quit.

CHAPTER 8:

FAITH

The next step to turning your minor setbacks into major come backs is keeping your faith strong. This step is so important that I am dedicating two chapters to it. There is a saying that goes, "First you make your habits and then your habits make you." If you want to be able to turn your minor setbacks into major comebacks, you need to start your day off with positive habits that empower you throughout the day. The problem is, for too many of us, we have negative habits in the morning, and we start our day off in a disempowered state that makes it unlikely that we will be able to deal with the potential setbacks of the day in a positive manner.

We are trained to think negatively when we wake up in the morning. When we wake up in the morning, most of us are awakened by an alarm clock. When something bad is happening, it is alarming. When there is a fire, an alarm goes off. When your house is broken into, an alarm goes off. There are very few alarms, if any, signifying positivity unless you win a prize on a game show, and we all know life is not a game show even though it is a game.

The alarm clock in the morning is training your mind and subconscious mind to associate waking up with negativity. No wonder so many of us wake up in a bad mood and have bad days. No wonder so many of us wake up with negative energy and negative mind states.

Because we are trained to associate waking up with negativity and something bad, but anybody in their right mind will acknowledge that waking up is in fact positive and a blessing.

It is rumored that Dr. King's morning ritual was coffee, orange juice, and then an hour of prayer and meditation. No wonder he was so powerful. No wonder he had so much faith. No wonder he could fight for and hold on to a dream no one could see. No wonder he was able to turn his setbacks into comebacks.

Jesus in his darkest hour was in the Garden of Gethsemane. He was about to face his biggest setback by going to the Cross. He asked his disciples to pray for him. As Jesus was praying, he found them sleeping. He then asked, "Could you not pray for an hour?" Sleep is what stopped the disciple from prayer and sleep is what stops us from prayer. We don't want to get up early and pray we would rather sleep. So, when the alarm clock goes off, we have just enough time to take a shower, get dressed, eat a meal, feed the kids, rush them off to school, and rush out the door. We begin our days wrong. We begin our days in a rush and in a hurry instead of in a powerful state of meditation and prayer. We start our days in alarm, with an alarm clock.

Notice that when it comes to all alarms, one of the major purposes of the alarm is to get you to rush. If a fire alarm goes off, the purpose is to get you to rush out the house because the house is on fire. Rushing is good when it comes to an emergency. When your house is on fire, you need to rush out the house to save your life. When your house is on fire, you should not try to save your laptop or the report that your boss wants done.

The problem is that because we are in a rush every morning, we forget things. The things we forget might not be laptops or reports. We forget to pray, we forget to meditate, we forget to read in the morning.

Therefore, we are not as productive on our jobs. Our family relationships suffer. We often say things to our children and spouse when we are rushing in the morning that can hurt their feelings and make them resentful. Instead of laptops, we forget love, joy, and peace. That's why we ought to get up early, pray, and read in the morning, so we won't be in a rush. It would help us in our careers, callings, and in our personal relationships.

Jesus said men out always to pray and faint not. See when you always pray, then you are not going to faint in the midst of a setback. When you pray, sometimes you will faint, give up, and cave in in the midst of a setback. When every day you always pray, you won't faint in the midst of a setback. The key word is always. How many of you always take a bath? You do it every day. How many of you always eat? You do it every day. How many of you always show up to work? You might not show up on time, but you always show up. How many of you always show up to work on time? See, the power of prayer is in the always. If you show up to work sometimes, you will be fired. If you do a good job sometimes, you will be fired. Prayer is like a job or anything else; the power is in what you do consistently, not what you do occasionally.

The reason we faint in the midst of setbacks is because we do not always pray; we pray sometimes. You might say, "I don't feel like praying, that's why I don't always pray." Well, you don't always feel like going to work, but you go. If you don't go, you will be unemployed. Some things you have to always do. See, when the Bible says men ought always to pray and faint not, that word faint means to give up, quit, throw in the towel, or lose hope.

In the Far East, the people plant a tree called the Chinese bamboo. During the first four years, they water and fertilize the plant everyday with seemingly little or no results. Then the fifth year again they apply water and fertilizer every day, and in five weeks, the tree grows ninety feet. The question is, did the tree grow ninety feet in five weeks or did it grow ninety feet in five years. The answer is, it grew ninety feet in five years. Because at any time during those five years, if the people had stopped watering the tree (fainted), it would have died. If the people would have said in the first year that all of this watering was not working and they don't see any results and therefore quit, the tree would have died. If they would have said that it is not working and they don't see any growth in the second year, the tree would have died. If they would have quit in the third year or the fourth year, the tree would have died. Sometimes you have to have faith that even when you don't see anything happening and it looks like it's not working, you have to keep going because that bamboo tree of yours is about to sprout up.

Many times, our dreams and plans appear not to be succeeding. We are tempted to give up and quit. Instead, we need to continue to water and fertilize those dreams and plans, nurturing the seeds of the vision God has placed within us. Because we know that if we do not quit, if we display perseverance and endurance, we will also reap a harvest.

I'm sure you have heard of Robert Kiyosaki, the author of the bestselling book *Rich Dad Poor Dad*, which has sold over twenty-two million copies. When he first wrote *Rich Dad Poor Dad*, he could not find a publisher. All publishers turned him down; they said they did not like the concept. They said he was a poor writer. They said the book did not make financial sense, and it would never sell. He was forced to self-publish his book. He sold his book by word of mouth, selling it to his friends and having them spread the word. He put up his own money to print one thousand books. The book eventually made it to the *New York Times* bestselling list, one of the few self-published books on the list. When it finally reached the *New York Times* bestselling list, Oprah called. He went on the Oprah Winfrey Show. Because of the show, the book eventually sold twenty-two million copies. It is rumored that he made $100 million in profit because he self-published his book, and the reason he self-published his book is because publishers turned him down. If he would have had a book deal, he would have only made a fraction of that.

Sometimes things that seem like curses can turn into blessings. None of this would have been possible if he would have given up when he faced a setback in the form of publishers rejecting him. Kiyosaki shares the story of how he faced a setback by going broke and was robbed of his money in a Velcro business by shady business partners. That experience is part of the reason he decided to write *Rich Dad Poor Dad*. The minor setback of him being robbed by his business partners turned into a major comeback in the form of him writing a book about financial intelligence that sold twenty-two million copies and counting. This book has helped millions of people become more financially intelligent, but this would not have happened without the setback caused by his shady business partners.

Blockbuster had the opportunity to buy a DVD mailing company called Netflix for $50 million in the year 2000. That might seem like a steep price tag, but it represented three days of blockbuster revenues. Netflix's value now stands at 32.9 billion, exceeding the value of CBS. Blockbuster missed an opportunity, and they have had plenty of company. Yahoo turned down the opportunity to acquire Google and Friendster turned down the opportunity to buy Facebook. If Blockbuster would have bought Netflix in its early stages, the owners of Netflix would not be as rich as they are today. If Friendster would have bought Facebook, Mark Zuckerberg would not be as rich as he is today. Sometimes, when things do not go our way or people do not believe in you and see your vision, it is a blessing in disguise. If record labels in New York would have given Jay-Z a deal, he would not have started his own record label and probably would not have become the first hip-hop billionaire.

It is a blessing when things don't go the way you planned and other people don't see your vision. Jay-Z had a plan for a record deal, but destiny had something bigger in store. Destiny wanted Jay-Z to become a boss. Just like Jay-Z, destiny has bigger things in store for each one of us. The key is, you should not get discouraged and give up when things don't go your way and people don't see your vision. I am sure the owners of Netflix's were disappointed when they did not get $50 million from Blockbuster, but they did not quit; now they are worth $32.9 billion and growing.

Some times when things don't happen right away, it's a blessing in disguise. That's why you should never quit when things don't work out your way. You should never let the opinions of others discourage you. You should never quit when you have a dream and people say no because even though people may say no, God is saying yes to your dream. If you want to turn a minor setback into a major comeback, you have to always remind yourself that man's rejection is God's protection. What other people think of you means nothing but what you think of yourself means everything.

CHAPTER 9:

FAITH IN ACTION

While I was in prison, I had a saying that I would constantly repeat to myself; as a matter of fact, not only did I say it to myself, I said it to anybody who would listen. I would say visualization, meditation, and affirmation is the combination to unlock manifestation. I will get into the specifics of what that means in another book. But when I would explain to my fellow inmates, a lot of them would say that they don't believe that one can make things manifest from the invisible.

They would tell me that they did not have faith and that they did not believe in anything they could not see. I would respond by saying that you can't see, touch, smell, or taste oxygen, but it is pumping through your lungs. You are breathing in oxygen, and without oxygen, you cannot survive. As a matter of fact, you can't see hydrogen or oxygen, but when you combine two parts hydrogen and one part oxygen, you get water, which covers around seventy-one percent of the Earth's surface. You cannot see, touch, smell, or taste gravity, but gravity keeps you from floating into space. There are G5, G6 waves that allow you to talk on your cell phone and use the Internet that are invisible to the naked eye. There are radio waves, infrared, ultraviolent, x-rays, and gamma rays that are invisible to the naked eye.

When Macaroni believed he could harness waves in order to have people talk to each other when they were not in the same vicinity, people thought he was crazy. Just like if you believe in faith, God, and prayer, some people will think you are crazy. But invincible forces run our lives. From cell phones, to the Internet, to oxygen, to gravity. To believe in this invisible force but to not to believe in the invisible creator who created these invisible forces is crazy. You have to use invisible forces to your advantage.

Just like the law of gravity is meant to keep you alive by keeping you from floating into space and dying, you can use the law of gravity to kill yourself by climbing on top of a building and jumping off the building. By jumping off a building, that invisible law of gravity will bring you down to your death. That invisible law of gravity was meant to keep you alive, but instead you used it intentionally or unintentionally to kill yourself. It's the same with electricity. Electricity can kill you, but electricity is meant to keep you warm in the winter. Keep you cool in the summer. Cook your food, wash your clothes. Electricity was put here to help us live a better life. The invisible law of belief is meant to help us manifest our goals, dreams, and desires that are not currently visible. But instead, a lot of us use the invisible law of belief to harm us. We believe that our children will get in trouble. We believe that our spouse is cheating on us. We believe we are not smart. We believe that something bad is going to happen to us. Our belief is fear-based, not faith-based.

Take for example Joshua and Caleb. They were two of the twelve spies who said that they can go up and possess the land. The other ten spies said they could not possess the land. That's life, you will find about ten out of twelve people are negative. You will find that about 80 percent of people will not believe in your dreams or theirs. You will find that 80 percent of people are negative. You will find that 80 percent of people are scared when faced with giant problems. You will find that about 80 percent of people have a negative self-image. You will find that 80 percent of people use their beliefs to manifest their fears instead of their hopes and dreams.

Out of the twelve spies, only two spies gave a good report. The rest, God said they gave an evil report. The report that God called evil was a report of doubt and unbelief. Out of the twelve spies, we only remember the names of two, Joshua and Caleb. If you want to be remembered, you need to be a person of faith. Of the twelve spies, only two spies entered the promised land, Joshua and Caleb. If you want to enter your promised land, you need to be a person of faith. If Jay-Z would have quit when all the record companies in New York turned him down, we would not have heard of him. If Mark Zuckerberg would have become discouraged and quit when Friendster did not see the vision of Facebook, we would not have heard of Mark Zuckerberg.

People of faith will be remembered. Martin Luther king Jr. was remembered because he was a person of faith and was not afraid to face the giants of racism and segregation. Susan B. Anthony is remembered because she was not afraid to face the giant of sexism. We are all called to stick out, not to fit in. We remember those that stick out and are not afraid to be themselves. Even though when you decide to be yourself, it will seem like the whole world is coming against you. Once you arrive, those same people who were against you will pat you on your back and say "I knew you could do it."

In order to get into your promised land and reach your goals, you will have to fight giants. The Bible says fight the good fight of faith. A good fight is a fight that we win. There is no victory without a fight. We talk about wanting victory, but there is no victory without being in a fight. We talk about overcoming, but you can't overcome without a struggle. We talk about winning, but you can't win unless there is a contest or a battle. We use all these phrases like "I am an overcomer" and "I am victorious." But then we get discouraged and want to complain and blame God when challenges arise. The irony in all of this is that you can't overcome without a challenge.

Let me tell you a secret: challenges will come if you have faith or not. Challenges will come if you are black or white, rich or poor, ugly or beautiful, smart or stupid. Life is full of challenges, but your faith determines whether you will be victorious or not. I was a politician for eight years, an effective politician, and I was able to accomplish so much because I was a fighter. I'm not bragging, but as a politician for eight years, I won every debate because I always got the last word. Ladies, can you testify when you are in a fight with your husband or boyfriend you are going to get the last word! Because when you are passionate about something, you are going to make sure you are heard and that you get the last word. If you don't get the last word, you go to bed angry and wake up arguing until you win that argument. A lot of politicians say they are fighters, but then when they are in a debate, they let the opposition get the last word. This proves they are not really fighting.

It is the same way with faith. When you are fighting the good fight of faith and thoughts come to your head that your business will not succeed, you cast those thoughts down. You say you are smart, competent, up to the task to succeed at any undertaking. In order to be a person of faith, you have to deal with negative self-talk. The Bible talks about casting down imaginations and bringing every thought into captivity. If a thought comes to your mind of fear, you have to tell yourself that you are as bold as a lion. If a thought comes to your head saying you should drop out of school, you have to tell yourself that you are not a quitter and that you will succeed in whatever you do. It can be thoughts of depression, thoughts of low self-esteem, pessimistic thoughts; whatever the thoughts are, you have to cast those thoughts down and replace them with positive thoughts.

It could be thoughts saying that you will be poor, broke, and never reach your dreams. You have to decide that you will always get the last word over negative thoughts and those last words will be positive affirmations that affirm your greatness and build confidence in your life. If you allow negative thoughts to go unchecked, you will eventually start to believe those negative thoughts of fear and failure. These thoughts will shape your destiny. As the Good Book says, "As a man thinketh in his heart so is he." So many people's lives and destiny are ruined because they cannot control their negative thoughts of fear. Then these negative thoughts of fear turn into a negative speech of fear and doubt. Negative thoughts and negative words destroy our faith.

The Good Book says that without faith, it is impossible to please God. Well, without faith, it is impossible to please anybody. If I say to you my name is Everette Witherspoon, and you don't believe me, you would be calling me a liar if you did not believe me. The Good Book says God is not a man that he should lie. So, when you say you don't believe God, you are calling him a liar. If I said I lived in a certain neighborhood, and you said you did not believe that I had the money or the credit to live in that neighborhood, that would not be pleasing to me. Because you are telling me you don't think I have the ability to afford that house. It's the same with God.

It is not pleasing to God when God tells you to start that business and you doubt God because you don't believe that he has the ability to make your business successful, despite your shortcomings. It is not pleasing to God when God tells you to go back to school or run for a political office and you doubt God because you don't believe he has the ability to work through you. You see yourself the way the children of Israel saw themselves as grasshoppers. You see yourself as someone too weak or not smart enough for God to use.

Now you might ask, how do you develop faith? How do you stay strong in hard times? The answer for me is a concept I call "No deposit, no withdrawal." That's the way it is in the banking system and that's the way it is in life. When you make deposits at the bank, you put the surplus money you have in the bank, and it's withdrawn when there is a need. That need could be a house payment, a car payment, or a payment of debt. You open a savings account to store your surplus, so you will have the money for a need. It could be to start a business, it could be a down payment on a house, or it could be the paying of a kid's tuition. You make deposits so you can make a withdrawal.

There are such things as spiritual and mental deposits you make into your life because there will be times when you will need to withdrawal from your reservoirs of spiritual and mental strength to overcome adversity. That's why you need to pray every day. You need to read inspirational and motivational books every day. You need to deposit strength within your spirit and your subconscious mind in order to withdraw it in the time of need. If a setback comes and you have not made the daily deposits of reading and praying, then you are likely to fold under that setback.

It takes discipline to read and pray daily. Just like it takes discipline to save your money instead of spending all the money you get. Some of us would rather spend time doing other things like watching TV all day, talking on the phone all day, staying on Instagram and Facebook all day, instead of reading and praying. Think about an insurance policy. If you have a house, you have homeowners' insurance. If you have a car, you have automobile insurance. If you have health care, you have health insurance. The thing about insurance is that you pray you don't need it, but you still make payments on your insurance policy.

It is the same way with mental and spiritual insurance. You hope you don't need to use it, but you pray daily; you read your Bible or other religious texts daily. You might practice visualization, affirmations, and meditations daily. You read from motivational and inspirational books daily. You listen to sermons from preachers or speeches from motivational speakers daily. I'm sure you would rather be watching TV, but you are making a deposit because you might need a withdrawal.

It's the same with insurance; you would rather spend that money on something else, but you spend it wisely on insurance, hoping you never need it. The reason why it's smart to pay that insurance is because in life, sooner or later, something happens. You might have a car and somebody hits your car, but guess what, since you have paid your insurance, you end up getting a brand-new car because you have paid your insurance; the car accident actually was a blessing in disguise. Your house was broken into. You might have had a TV that was five years old, a couch that was twelve years old; these items were stolen, but because you had insurance, you got a brand-new TV, brand-new couch, brand-new furniture, brand-new everything.

When you pay your spiritual insurance, when calamity strikes, you end up coming out of that calamity, coming out of that setback better than ever. People used to ask me in prison, "How are you so positive? How do you maintain such hope? Why are you smiling?" I even smiled in my mugshots. I would tell them because I have made spiritual and mental deposits, so I can make spiritual and mental withdrawals during the hard times. I would tell them I have paid my spiritual and mental insurance, so I'm coming out brand-new. I'm turning this minor setback into a major comeback.

CHAPTER 10:

THE SPOKEN WORD

The next step in turning a minor setback into a major comeback is understanding and utilizing the power of the spoken word. The year of 1996 is a year I will never forget for several reasons. The first reason is because I graduated high school in 1996. The second reason is that the professional careers of two legends were started in 1996. One in basketball being Kobe Bryant, and the other in music being Jay- Z.

In 1996, when Kobe Bryant said that he was going to be one of the greatest to play basketball, I thought he was crazy. There were a lot of young players that were better than him in 1996 Allen Iverson and Shaq, to name a few. He was not even starting on his own team, but he proved doubters wrong because he believed in himself. In 1996, Jay-Z came on the scene with reasonable doubts. He talked a lot of big talk on that album, saying he was going to take over rap. Even though the album was a classic, a lot of people thought he was crazy when he said he was going to take over rap and become the greatest. In 1996, there were a lot of rappers hotter than Jay-Z. Biggie, Tupac, and Snoop Dog, to name a few. Jay-Z eventually proved the world wrong by becoming arguably the greatest rapper of all time and the first hip-hop billionaire, because he believed in himself.

The year of 1996 is a year I will never forget for another reason. In 1996, one of the greatest rappers of all time, Tupac was shot and killed on the Las Vegas Strip. Then in March of 1997, another one of the greats Biggie Smalls was killed. The death of Tupac and Biggie to my generation was just as tragic as the death of Martin Luther king Jr. and Malcom X was for previous generations.

Before Tupac, you hardly ever saw African Americans with tattoos; now everybody has tats including CEOs, bankers, politicians, and preachers. Biggie was the best lyricist and storyteller rap has ever seen. Tupac and Biggie were just as great as Jay Z, if not greater. They had the same ambition as Jay-Z, if not more. They had the same work ethic as Jay-Z, if not a greater work ethic. They had the same talent as Jay-Z, if not greater talent. Their music was just as good as Jay-Z's music, if not better. What separated Jay-Z from Biggie and Tupac were his words.

Proverbs 18:21 says life and death are in the power of the tongue. Jay Z rapped and talked about life, the good life. Tupac and Biggie talked about death. Tupac had songs like "If I die 2nite." Tupac invented the term "Ryde or Die." Tupac always talked about getting shot. Biggie's first album was called *Ready to Die*. Biggie's second album was called *Life After Death*, but Jay-Z had songs like "Can I live." Jay-Z had albums called *In my Lifetime* Volumes 1, 2, and 3. Jay-Z spoke the good life and got it. Biggie and Tupac spoke death and got it.

Sean Combs is another great example of the power of the spoken word. Sean Combs made it cool to be a boss. Before Sean Combs, a lot of young African Americans were not thinking about owning their own business. Sean Combs made being the boss and CEO mainstream. Sean Combs was the first example of an African American man as a CEO in mainstream media. He made being a CEO cool.

There were plenty of African American CEOs before Sean Combs: Bob Johnson, Barry Gordy, and Don Cornelius, to name a few. But Sean Combs was the first African American CEO mainstream celebrity that bragged about being a boss. People who really know Sean Combs know that he has a motto that he lives his life by. That motto is "Can't stop, won't stop."

Why does Sean Combs the music mogul keep saying "I can't stop, won't stop"? Because it's an affirmation that helps him turn his setbacks into comebacks. In 1991, nine people were trampled to death at a concert Sean Combs threw at City College in New York. This tragedy and setback would have stopped and destroyed most people's careers, but it could not stop him. Later in his career, Sean Combs faced another setback by getting fired from Uptown Records where he started the careers of Jodeci and Mary J. Blige. He was fired for talking crazy and having a big head. That setback would have stopped and destroyed most people's careers, but it could not stop him.

He came back and started Bad Boy Records. He built Bad Boy Records into the biggest record label in music. Then he suffered another setback, his best friend Biggie Smalls and the biggest rap artist at the time, possibly the best ever, was murdered. This type of setback would have stopped most people and destroyed their careers, but it could not stop Sean Combs. Some years later, he was dating Jenifer Lopez, the biggest pop star at the time. Sean Combs got her caught in an attempted murder case with him. He was on trial and could have served ten years in prison. Sean Combs' biggest artists at the time, the rapper he was going to rebuild Bad Boy records around, Shyne, was sentenced to ten years in prison because of his involvement in the incident.

This tragedy and setback would have stopped most people and destroyed their careers, but not Sean Combs. Sean Combs just faced the biggest setback of his life, that being the death of the mother of four of his children, Kim Porter, but he is still going strong. Andrea Harrell, his mentor that gave him his first opportunity in the music business, recently died but he is still going strong. He is now richer and more successful than ever, so when he says he can't stop, won't stop, he really means it.

Muhammad Ali stated, "I said I was the greatest. I said that before I knew I was." When Ali said he was going to beat Sonny Listen, people thought he was crazy. When he said he was going to beat George Foreman, people thought he was crazy. When you stand up and say that you are going to fulfill your dreams, people are going to say you are crazy. When you are positive and still motivated at the midnight hour of your life, people are going to think you are crazy.

Now everybody does not have the confidence or the ego of a Kobe Bryant, Jay-Z, Sean Combs, or Muhammad Ali. Nevertheless, we can all have faith to fulfill our individual callings and turn our setbacks into comebacks. When Stallone refused to take the $150,000 for the movie script, people thought he was crazy. When Stallone said he wanted to act, agents thought he was crazy. When Barrack told people that he wanted to be president, people thought he was crazy.

When you decide to follow your dreams or rise above mediocrity, people will think you are crazy, even people who love you. Even Tyler Perry's mother told him to quit writing plays and get a job. I could see her now, telling her son Tyler Perry who is six foot-five inches tall, why are you dressing up in a dress like a woman? Why are you putting on makeup and wearing heels? You need to take that wig off, quit wasting your time and get a job. She could not see his vision. She could not see how those plays would make him a billionaire and open up opportunities for so many African Americans in the acting industry.

If he would have listened to his mother, who I'm sure loves him, he would probably be working at Walgreens or Rite Aid today. See, it can be your mother, father, or spouse who is trying to talk you out of your dreams. It can be your mother, father, siblings, or spouse that tries to make you give up in the midst of a setback. The fact is that it is your dream, not your parent's or your spouse's. If you are laughed at, ridiculed, or doubted for following your dreams, you are not alone; all the greats have this in common. That's why it so important to have positive self-talk, because even though other people are telling you that you will never make it, what matters most in life is what you say about your situation, what are you saying about your life, what is coming out of your mouth.

What comes out of your mouth has the power to transform your life. Look at the caterpillar. The cocoon that transforms it into the butterfly comes out of the caterpillar's mouth. Your cocoon that will transform your life from one of a caterpillar to one of a butterfly is formed by what comes out of your mouth. Think about caterpillars: they crawl, but butterflies fly. You can go from crawling to flying by what comes out of your mouth.

Think about caterpillars: they are ugly, but butterflies are beautiful. Your life can go from ugly to beautiful by what comes out of your mouth. Think about caterpillars: they are despised but butterflies are admired; you can go from being despised to being admired by what comes out of your mouth. You can go from a minor setback to a major comeback by what comes out of your mouth.

A lot of us, when we speak something, we expect it to manifest instantly. Sometimes this can be the case, but there are times when it actually looks like things are getting worse, not better, when you are speaking things into existence. Think about the caterpillar: the cocoon comes from its mouth, but being in a cocoon is worse than being a caterpillar. The caterpillar before it goes into a cocoon has freedom of movement and actually makes some progress, even though the movement is very slow and the progress is minimum. When the caterpillar goes into the cocoon, all the progress stops; it is in a dark place.

Sometimes when you are speaking things into existence, it will appear as if you are going into a dark place because that's where a lot of our transformations occur, in a dark place. Photographs are developed in the dark, not in the light. That internal picture of what you want your life to become will be developed in the dark, not in the light. You might be alone for a while, but transformation occurs more when you are by yourself than with a group of people. Sometimes your elevation requires isolation. The important thing is that during the dark times, if you want to turn your setbacks into comebacks, you have to keep speaking things into existence; you should not give up during the process. The caterpillar being inside the cocoon is a minor setback, but the caterpillar turning into a butterfly is a major comeback.

The thing about being in a cocoon that is a setback for the caterpillar is that the caterpillar, when it is in the cocoon, has to trust the process. Likewise, when we are speaking positive words, and it looks like things are getting worse, we need to trust the process. There was a story about a young kid who saw a butterfly struggling to breakout out of its cocoon. The butterfly had one wing out and was struggling to break through the cocoon to get the other wing out. The young boy had pity on the butterfly and took out his pocket knife. The young boy decided to cut the butterfly out of the cocoon. When the boy did this, the butterfly instantly fell to the ground and died. In fact, it was not even a fully developed butterfly. The butterfly only had one wing. The butterfly was half butterfly and half caterpillar because the butterfly's wings were to be developed by struggling to break through the cocoon.

The process of the butterfly fighting to break through the cocoon is what develops the butterfly's wings and gives the butterfly strength to fly. When you are making affirmations, don't give up during the process and don't let people come around and fill your mind with thoughts of self-pity. You can't be pitiful and powerful at the same time. Never indulge in self-pity. Indulge in self-power. You have reservoirs of power in yourself, and affirmations and positive self-talk is one of the best ways to bring that power out. It is okay, as a matter fact, it is good for others to help you, which is a positive thing, but for others to pity you is a negative thing.

When God saw darkness, he said let there be light, and that started the universe as we know it. God is the creator, and we are made in the image and likeness of God. God created the world by speaking. God said then he saw. We have that same power to speak and see what we speak eventually materialize in our lives. Just like God, we can use our words to create our worlds. The spoken word created the universe, and the universe responds to the spoken word. What you get from the universe will come from your spoken words. Don't use your words to describe the situation; use your words to change the situation.

Acts 16:25 says, "And at midnight Paul and Silas prayed and sang praises to God, and the prisoners heard them." Notice Paul and Silas were shackled up; they had just been beaten. Their backs were bleeding, but they did not complain. They sang praises to God. Notice that it was at midnight. Midnight is a metaphor for the darkest time in your life. It was dark; Paul and Silas were going to be put to death. They did not complain and say "God, why did you let this happen? "Nothing ever works out for me." "Life is so unfair." "I am so unlucky." "I never get any good breaks." If they would have talked like that at the darkest point in their lives, they would never have escaped prison, they probably would have been executed the next morning. But instead, they chose to praise God, and the reason so many of our dreams die is because we complain and get into self-pity when it is dark in our lives.

Notice Paul and Silas: they praised the Lord, and the prisoners heard it and their chains were loosened. When you are grateful and when you speak positive words in the face of the direst circumstance, you will get the victory if you believe. Notice that they praised God, and the prisoners heard it. I'm sure the prisoners thought that Paul and Silas were crazy because they were singing and praising God when they were locked up. I'm sure the prisoners were thinking to themselves, you are locked up, God can't hear you in here. I'm sure the prisoners were thinking, do you know you are about to die, it is midnight, there is no hope for you.

I am sure when Jay-Z was turned down by every record label in New York, it seemed like his dream was dead. I'm sure those were dark times for him, but he continued to make music. He continued to say that he was the best. He continued to stay positive, and he spoke life into his dead dreams. When he saw darkness, he said let there be light. Dr. Dre, one of the most successful music producers of all time, went broke when N.W.A. broke up because he had no record deal. He tried to sell his new record *The Chronic* to every major record label in the music business; they all turned him down. I'm sure at that time, his dreams seemed dead. I'm sure at that time in his life it was dark, but he persisted. He continued to shop his record, and it was eventually picked up by an upstart record label Interscope, and by his persistence, positive thoughts, and words, he spoke life into his dead dreams.

I myself faced a tax evasion charge that could have landed me in prison for ten years and actually landed me in prison for a year. I did not think it was right, and it was not right. It was a politically motivated charge. It was dark in my life. But like God, when I saw darkness, I said let there be light.

Even if you don't believe in God, or you believe in God but not the Bible, you still have to recognize the power of your words. Think of Neuro Linguistic Programming (NLP). Neuro means mind, linguistic means language, and program is to control. It is the science of using words to program and control your mind.

Think of Fidel Castro when he was in the jungles of Cuba, on the run from Batista's army. Two-thirds of Fidel's army had been killed by Batista's army. Fidel Castro had fifteen men left alive. He kept saying to his troops while on the run in the jungle that "We are winning." That they were going to run this country. He had so much faith in the spoken word that he even gave seven of his fifteen men ranks in his army and cabinet positions in his new administration right there in the jungle.

I'm sure his followers thought he was crazy. I am sure his soldiers thought in the back of their minds that there were only seventeen of them and there was no way Fidel was ever going be the leader of Cuba. I'm sure the soldiers thought that there was no way that they were going to make it out the jungle alive. I'm sure it was a dark time in Fidel's life, but in less than two weeks from that time, he was the leader of Cuba. No matter what you think about Castro, when he saw darkness, just like God, he said, "Let there be light." Somebody might say that Castro, Jay-Z, and Dr. Dre are not people of faith. I don't know if they are people of faith or not, but when they saw darkness in their life, just like God, they said, "Let there be light."

Too many people when they have bad circumstances, when their dreams seem dead, they go into self-pity, they become negative, they become afraid. They murmur and complain and say, "Why me, Lord?" Murmuring and complaining will keep you from fulfilling your dreams. Skeptics and critics say that when you talk faith, you are denying that there is a problem. No, we are not denying problems; we are defying problems. We are not denying hard times; we are defying hard times. Problems might be in our lives, but they will not defeat us.

We have to come to the realization that, what is happening when our dreams are not manifesting as fast as we want them to is that our faith is being tested to see how bad do, we want what is rightfully ours. You are being tested to see if you have the faith to fulfill your destiny. If you want your circumstances to turn around, you have to turn your words around. When somebody tells you no, you have to turn that word no around. When you turn no around, you get on. As in keep on, press on, move on, because in order to change your situation around, you have to keep moving and keep pressing on.

People of faith don't stop. When something evil or bad happens to you, whether it's a death in the family, whether it's a sickness, whether it is financial hardship, betrayal, etc., you have to turn that word evil around in order to turn that situation around. When you turn the word evil around, you get the word live. You have to decide that you are going to live on. You have to decide you are going to live more fully. You have to decide that you are going to live happier. You have to decide you are going to live with more joy, live with more peace, live with more fulfilment. People of faith turn their words around, and that's how they turn their worlds around. That's how they turn their circumstances around. That's how they turn minor setbacks into major comebacks.

CHAPTER 11:

FEAR

The next step in turning a minor setback into a major comeback is learning how to deal with fear because when you are going through a setback, it can be very scary. If you don't know how to appropriately respond to fear, then fear will keep you from turning your setback into a comeback. Have you ever watched a great fighter like Muhammad Ali? He would call his opponents like Sonny Liston ugly, slow, and weak. He would tell Sonny Liston that he is going to beat him in three rounds. He would say that he would beat Sonny Liston so bad that he would have to retire. After he beat Sonny Liston, he would tell other fighters, "I'm going to beat you worse than Sonny Liston."

All of this talking was designed to put fear in his opponent's heart. The same with Rick Flair; he would tell his opponents he was going to whip them before the fight or at the press conference. The same with Hulk Hogan. The same with Mike Tyson, Sugar Ray Leonard, Floyd Mayweather, etc. All great fighters do it.

Here is the thing we all need to recognize: we are all fighters and we are all in a fight whether we know it or not. Whether we are winning the fight or not, we are in a fight. We have adversaries, and those adversaries talk to us just like Ali talked to Sonny Liston, telling us they will defeat us. Telling us we will not make it. Telling us we should give up, telling us there is no hope. These adversaries can even be our own thoughts, fears, and doubts.

Think about David. Every day, the giant Goliath came down to the battlefield and spoke blasphemies to the army of Israel. When David heard it, he said, "Who is this uncircumcised Philistine that he speaks blasphemies to the army of the living God?" Just like the Giant Goliath talked to the army of Israel to make them afraid, giant problems will talk to you to make you afraid. You can have cancer, and that cancer will tell you "I'm going to kill you." You can be fired from your job, and that giant of debt will tell you that you are going to lose your house and your car. You can be in a relationship and that giant of jealousy will tell you your significant other is cheating on you. The giant of loneliness will tell you that nobody loves you. The giant of depression will tell you to kill yourself. The giant of insecurity will tell you that you are ugly and stupid.

Notice David heard the giant and responded with faith. In order for David to reach his destiny and to turn his setback into a comeback, he had to go through that giant. In order for the children of Israel to reach the promised land, they had to go through giants. In order for you to fulfill your calling, reach a new level, and turn your setbacks into comebacks, you will have to face your giants.

I believe David was a lot like Muhammad Ali, or should I say Muhammad Ali was a lot like David. People thought David was arrogant. People thought Ali was arrogant. Ali told you what he was going to do, and he did it. David told you what he was going to do, and he did it. The people loved David, and the people loved Ali. The powers that be hated David and Ali. David was on the run, living in caves, and Ali was stripped of his title. Both were underdogs. Both Ali and David used their words and actions to overcome fear.

In order to be able to turn your setbacks into comebacks, you have to be able to deal with fear and act in the face of fear. When you look at the Bible, Saul was appointed and anointed to be the first King of Israel. The first thing that Saul did when he became king is that he hid from the people because he was afraid. Fear will stop you from being a great leader. Because of Saul's fear, God chose David to be king instead of Saul.

After David was anointed king, you read about David going to the battle and challenging Goliath, the leader of the Philistine army who were persecuting Israel. The first thing Saul does is try to talk David out of attacking Goliath, saying that he could not defeat Goliath because he was just a youth and Goliath was a man of war since his youth. Notice how people who are scared will try to make you scared and discourage you from fulfilling your destiny. David did not listen to Saul. He attacked the giant Goliath and ended up slaying Goliath.

Everybody who has become great and made a significant impact on their generation had to face and slay the giant of fear. Think of General George Washington, who would eventually become this country's first president. He ordered that a fifteen-foot statue of King George the Third be torn down. His troops tore down the statue, broke the statue into pieces, and melted the pieces into 42,088 bullets. George Washington then commanded his army to shoot these bullets at King George the Third's red coat army. That statue of King George was a sign of oppression.

That statue of King George was put there to strike fear into the hearts of the colonists. The statue was put there to tell the people of the thirteen colonies that King George is the king of England, the most powerful country in the world. The giant of the world. The Goliath of the world. Notice that if George Washington would have bowed down to fear, there would be no United States of America. George Washington did not listen to King George; he tore down that statue and attacked the red coats. Sometimes you have to attack fear. The whole purpose of the statue was to put fear in the hearts of the colonists to keep them from taking action. Fear keeps you from taking action, and action is what changes things.

The Bible says the devil walks about as a roaring lion seeking whom he may devour. The lion roars to paralyze its prey with fear. When the prey is paralyzed, it can't move and is devoured by the lion. The devil uses his voice just like a lion to paralyze you with fear. He tells you that you can't make it to paralyze you. He tells you that you will die of sickness to paralyze you. He tells you that you are not smart enough to paralyze you, to keep you from taking action and reaching your goals. The devil is the father of lies and tells you that you are not good enough to make you quit.

Faith without works is dead and nothing changes without action. The devil's whole purpose of acting like a roaring lion is to paralyze you with fear so you will never take action. So that you will never make progress. So that you will never enter your promised land. So that you will never fulfill your destiny, and thereby making sure you are stuck in the same place all of your life because you are too afraid to act.

It says over eighty times in the Bible, "Fear not." Anytime somebody tells you something over eighty times, they are trying to tell you something. As a matter fact, "fear not" is the most repeated command in the Bible. It's a phrase that is used in both the New Testament and the Old Testament. The reason why is that everybody has to deal with fear, and fearful thoughts are what keep us from taking action.

Think about this before you decide to entertain fearful thoughts. Every cell in your body is connected to your heart. Your heart is controlled by your brain. Your brain is controlled by your mind. The way you think literally controls every cell in your body. That's what the Bible means by "As a man thinketh in heart so is he." That's what the Bible means when it says, "Be not conformed to this world but be ye transformed by the renewing of your mind." Your thoughts literally transform you from the inside out. Thoughts don't just deal with the metaphysical, they also deal with the physical. Negative thoughts of fear can actually cause disease and depression. Negative thoughts of fear can cause a heart attack, stroke, you name it. Negative thoughts and worry can actually kill you. Jesus commanded his disciples to be anxious for nothing. Worry and anxiety kill people. Those thoughts of stress and strain cause physical damage to your body. Those fearful thoughts can cause you to have a stroke.

Franklin D. Roosevelt said it best, "There is nothing to fear but fear itself." We all acknowledge the greatness of Franklin D. Roosevelt, and he is widely acknowledged as one of the greatest presidents in this nation's history. A major part of his great success, and some people will say the main part of his success, was his wife, Eleanor. Eleanor Roosevelt had her own fight with fear, which she had to overcome in order to develop into the woman who would eventually redefine what it means to be the first lady of the United States. One of Eleanor's Roosevelt's most famous quotes is, "You gain strength, courage, and confidence by every experience in which you really stop to look fear in the face. You are able to say to yourself, 'I lived through this horror. I can take the next thing that comes along.'"

Eleanor Roosevelt was born into upper class New York society in 1884. Her mother, Anna, was a society beauty who was cold toward her plain-looking daughter. Her father Elliot adored Eleanor, and she adored him. He was a popular man but had a drinking problem. While her father was sent to a clinic for recovering alcoholics, her mother

Anna grew ill and died of diphtheria. Six months later, Eleanor's four-year-old brother died. Because of these setbacks, Eleanor's father Elliot started having more severe battles with depression, drugs, and alcohol. He died a few months before her tenth birthday. He was the center of her world, and his death left her devastated. The setbacks from her painful childhood would leave her with an empathy for those who were suffering that was basic to her personality and achievement.

Eleanor was sent to boarding school in England. She would eventually come back to the United States. When she was twenty-one, she married Franklin D. Roosevelt. If you are wondering, they were distant cousins, but never mind that. For the next twelve years, Eleanor was a wife and a mother, having six children, one of which died in infancy. In the thirteenth year of her marriage, her world was shattered when she discovered that her husband FDR was having an affair with her secretary. She was deeply saddened and depressed, but she decided to stay in her marriage.

Her courage and faith were tested again in 1921 when the family was staying at their holiday home in Maine. FDR had been swimming and that night felt tired. The next day, he could not move his legs; he had been stricken with polio and would not walk properly again. In 1933, FDR would become president of the United States. Now the Democratic Party is considered the political party of women's rights and the party that women are more likely to be affiliated with, but it was not like that before Eleanor Roosevelt; more women were Republicans. In the presidential race of 1932, she created a group called the grass trampers who were instrumental in increasing female support for the Democrats. Eleanor Roosevelt held the first ever press conference for a wife of the president and invited only women to it. She published a feminist-leaning book *It's up to the women*.

Eleanor became FDR's eyes and ears going out into the country to see the overwhelming poverty and joblessness that had overwhelmed the nation. Her desires to bond with housewives, mineworkers, soldiers, and struggling farmers and to make friends with black and Jewish Americans would make her seem like a bleeding heart to opponents and a traitor to her class. But her nose for suffering and oppression made her a much-loved figure for many ordinary people. She was able to empathize instead of just offering sympathy.

ER gave strong support to improvements in labor laws and contributed to the foundation of the Civil Rights Movement by highlighting the lynching that was still taking place in the South. She enjoyed entertaining prominent African Americans at the White House. This was unheard of at the time. When her friend Marian Anderson, the great American contralto, tried to book a concert in Washington DC at a hall owned by the daughters of the American Revolution, this organization refused to let African Americans perform. In protest, Eleanor, a long-time member, resigned and helped organize a huge concert for Anderson at the Lincoln memorial. The black voters that Eleanor attracted away from the Republicans are still with the Democratic Party till this day.

The reason Eleanor Roosevelt was known as the best first lady in history at that time. The reason she was so compassionate and had so much empathy was because of what she had been through in her life, the tragedy of her whole family dying, surviving affairs, and the illness of FDR. Her worst fears came true, and she survived all of them. All of this made her a more compassionate first lady. ER faced minor setbacks, but she turned them into major comebacks not just for herself but also for the downtrodden people in the United States of America.

CHAPTER 12:

READING

The next step to turning your minor setbacks into major comebacks is developing a daily habit of reading. Seneca, the famous Roman philosopher, said it best when he stated books are the training weights of the mind. The stronger your mind is, the more likely you will be able to turn a minor setback into a major comeback. If you want to become a millionaire, you will have to overcome a lot of setbacks. The average black millionaire reads two books a month. That is twenty-four books a year and 240 books in ten years. The average black middle-class person reads about two books a year. The average black person in poverty reads about two books in their lifetime. The average black prison inmate can't read; they are illiterate.

According Nielsen Wire, the global leader in consumer insights, the average African American household spends more than seven hours each day, 40 percent more than the overall population, and nearly nine times that of the average black millionaire, watching television. As stated before, wealthy African Americans, however, read nearly two books a month, twenty-four books a year. Ask yourself, did you read twenty-four books last year? And are you on track to read twenty-four books this year? When we watch TV, we always see commercials, and a lot of those commercials are automobile commercials. We see commercials for Toyota, Jeep, Honda, Acura, etc. We even see commercials for Mercedes and BMW. But we never see commercials for Lamborghini, Ferrari, Bentley, and Rolls Royce. The reason why is because people that have the money to afford these automobiles do not watch a lot of TV.

Sixty percent of all prison inmates are functionally illiterate. Prison records show that prison inmates who receive literacy help have a 16 percent rate of recidivism. Inmates who do not receive help with literacy have a 70 percent chance of recidivism. It is proven that one of the most effective ways for a former prisoner to turn the minor setback of incarceration into a major comeback is through reading. Prisons are built based on third-grade reading and math scores. There are currently more Africans Americans in prison, on probation, or on parole than there were African Americans enslaved during the height of slavery in 1860. The wicked system of slavery depended on a lot of things, but one of the main things it depended on was making sure that slaves were illiterate.

Fredrick Douglas said that the ability to read and write is the first step toward freedom. Fredrick Douglas stated that education means emancipation. When Fredrick Douglas learned to read, he developed a defiant attitude toward the master, which eventually led to his freedom. He loved to read so much that his master tried to beat him and hang him because he would read all day and not work hard like the rest of the slaves. When Fredrick Douglas's master tried to beat him, it came to his mind that his master would kill him so he needed to fight back. Fredrick Douglas ended up fighting his master for thirty minutes; after the fight, he was exhausted, and his master was lying on the ground bleeding.

Fredrick Douglas's master let him go. His master had a reputation of breaking slaves without killing them, because during that time, if you killed a slave, you would be losing money on an investment. Fredrick Douglas's master said we need to let him go because his mind is too strong to be broken. See, when you are free in your mind, it's going to manifest on the outside. Fredrick Douglas read about being a statesman when he was a slave. In his mind, he was already a statesman even though he was a slave on a slave plantation. So, it was just a matter of time before his inward vison of himself manifested and changed his outward circumstances.

Also, when you read and develop your mind and your mind becomes stronger, just like Fredrick Douglas, you will develop a defiant attitude. You will develop a defiant attitude against the odds. You will start to defy the odds. Just like in Fredrick Douglas's time, it was unlikely that a slave would gain his freedom, but he did, and it all started when he started to read.

The odds may be against you to become a successful businessman, but because you read, you defy the odds. The odds might be against you to become a millionaire, but because you read on finances, you defy the odds. The odds might be against you to win that election and become a big-time politician, but you defy the odds. The odds might be against you to rise up the corporate ladder, but because you read, you defy the odds. Because you are a reader, you develop a defiant attitude just like Fredrick Douglas did. Because you are a reader, you start to see yourself as successful no matter what your current situation is. Because you are a reader, you start to focus on your destination, not your situation.

The Bible called Joseph prosperous even though he was a slave. You have to be prosperous on the inside before it manifests on the outside. Reading changes the way you see yourself. Hosea 4:6 says, "My people are destroyed for a lack of knowledge. Because thou has rejected knowledge, I will also reject thee. That thou shall be no priest to me, seeing thou hast forgotten the law of thy God, I will also forget thy children."

It is important that we read to gain knowledge. But so many of us have rejected knowledge. Knowledge for most people is more easily attainable now than any time in history. Think about Fredrick Douglas. He would read even though reading a book meant that he could possibly face death. Slaves like him and Booker T. Washington learned how to read even though it meant that they could possibly be beaten or put to death.

Nowadays, we refuse to read books. During the time Hosea the prophet wrote this scripture, there were probably a lot of illiterate people. Books were probably hard to come by. I'm pretty sure there were no public libraries or a public education system to teach people to read, at least not like the ones we have today. There was a time during the Dark Ages when no books were allowed to be printed. During slavery, it was illegal to teach slaves to read. We now live in a time when you don't even have to know how to read; there are plenty of audio books. You can check out audio books from the library. You can listen to audio books on YouTube. There is no excuse not to have knowledge in this information age, but we still reject knowledge.

Not having knowledge affects our children. When parents don't have an education, whether it be a college education or simply being financially educated, they are less likely to have a good job or a successful business. They are less likely to have the credit or the capital to buy a home in a nice neighborhood. The neighborhood you live in determines the quality of school your child goes to. The quality of education determines what college your child goes to. The college your child goes to determines the job your child gets, and the cycle repeats itself with your grandchildren. If you are unemployed or living in poverty, it is more likely that your child will live in poverty and become locked up, and that cycle repeats itself. That is why it is important to seek knowledge; it not only helps you; it also helps your children.

Think of Malcom X. Somebody asked Malcom X, "What is your alma mater?" He said books. It is rumored that when Malcom X was incarcerated, he read for fifteen hours a day and that he read just about every book in the prison library. We see the pictures and videos of Malcom X wearing glasses, but when he was first arrested, he had perfect 20/20 eye sight. While he was in prison, he read a lot of books. A lot of the books he read in the dark; the only light he had was the light in the hallway outside his cell. He wore out his eyes so bad that he had to wear glasses. By reading books in prison, he lost his eyesight, but he gained his vision.

He said if he had a free fifteen minutes, he spent it studying. All great leaders have a hunger to read. Reading is a mental exercise that makes your mind strong. As a matter of fact, you don't see with your eyes; you see through your eyes. You see with your mind. Readers see plans, possibilities, and strategies that others don't see. When you read the right books, you will gain wisdom, inspiration, and most importantly, hope. This wisdom, inspiration, and hope you gain from reading will help you turn your setbacks into comebacks.

As stated before, vison is not seen with the eyes; vision is seen with the mind. If you want 20/20 vison, which is great vision, try reading twenty books this year. With vision, you see what is not apparent to the naked eye. When you have vision, you see possibilities that can happen that have not materialized. If you want to improve your vision when it comes to finances, challenge yourself to read twenty books on finance this year. I bet you will have 20/20 vision in your finances. If you want to stay motivated to achieve your goals, read twenty books on motivation this year. I bet you will have 20/20 vison when it comes to achieving your goals. The same with your faith, your health, leadership skills, and your career. If you dedicate yourself to read twenty books a year on the particular subject you want to make improvements in, I guarantee you that you will see radical change in that area of your life. I guarantee you that you will gain 20/20 vision in that area.

Notice Malcom X loved to read books but not newspapers. He said reading the newspaper will have you hating the oppressed and loving the oppressor. You won't find any spiritual teacher or any faith teacher encouraging you to read the newspaper every day. You won't find any motivational speaker, life coach, or self-help guru encouraging you to read the newspaper. The newspaper is about the negative extremes: a man is murdered, a house is burned down, a scandal happened; they report some good, but it is quickly drowned out by the negative. About 80 percent of the news written or aired is negative and 20 percent of news, if that much, is positive.

Even in politics, elected officials who are strong and create policy that impacts people's lives for the better read a lot of books on policy. They don't let the newspapers and media shape the way they think. See, if you don't read anything, you will be uninformed, but if you just read the newspaper, it is likely that you will be misinformed. It's funny that during Covid-19, at first, they kept the liquor stores open because they said they were essential, but the book stores were closed because they were not essential. Knowledge is always essential, and reading is always essential for us to grow, especially if we are to turn our minor setbacks into major comebacks.

CHAPTER 13:

READ MORE

When in the midst of a minor setback, it is important to read positive motivational nonfiction books that help you grow and mature as a person, so that you will be able to turn your minor setback into a major comeback. There is a famous saying that goes: you are going to be the same person you are today five years from now except for two things, the people you hang around and the books you read. See, we don't decide our future; we decide our habits, and our habits decide our future. Will Smith says two Rs make him successful, and no they are not rest and relaxation. They are reading and running. He says he exercises his mind by reading and exercises his body by running. Les Brown, arguably the greatest motivational speaker ever, said his life began to change when he started reading thirty minutes a day.

Bill Gates reads fifty books a year, that averages out to about a book a week. It was said of Bill Gates that when he was a student at Harvard, he read books on business like other male students read Playboy magazine. By the way, Playboy magazine was very popular back then. When some people tell the story of Bill Gates, they label him as a college dropout. The difference between Bill Gates and most college dropouts is that most college dropouts quit school because they don't like to read or study. Bill Gates loved to read so much and gained so much knowledge by reading that he did not have to finish college. He already had enough knowledge to start Microsoft without finishing college.

The average CE0 of a Fortune 500 company reads about fifty-two books a year. That's a book a week. Warren Buffet said when he was starting his investment career, he would read six hundred to a thousand pages a day. Till this day, he estimates that he spends 80 percent of his time reading. You might say a book a week is a lot of reading; well, these people that usually read a book a week have a lot of money, have a lot of success, and have turned a lot of setbacks into comebacks because they have a lot of knowledge.

The Bible says wisdom is the principal thing. The Good Book says to seek wisdom. When you read a book a week, you are seeking wisdom. To the average person, reading a book a week sounds like a lot of reading, but to the person who reads a book a week, watching six to eight hours of TV a day sounds like a lot of wasted time. By the time the average American is sixty years old, he or she has watched fifteen years' worth of TV. To a person who reads a book a week, spending three to four hours on the phone gossiping seems like a lot of wasted time. To a person who reads a book a week, spending three to four hours a day on social media, unless you are promoting your business or a cause you are passionate about, seems like a lot of wasted time.

To a person who reads a book a week, spending five to six hours a day playing video games seems like a lot of wasted time. We all have twenty-four hours in a day; the successful people use the majority of their twenty-four hours seeking knowledge and taking action. To some people, reading a book a week might be extreme, but in order to be successful, you have to be extreme because reaching one's goals, fulfilling one's destiny, and reaching one's purpose can be extremely difficult if one is not totally committed.

Most successful people know that if you do things casually, then you will be a casualty. That's why they live by the motto of "Go hard or go home." The reason why Warren Buffet read six hundred to a thousand pages on investing a day is because he wanted to be the best investor. He wanted to know everything about investing. So that when financial setbacks occurred, he would have the knowledge to turn those setbacks into comebacks. Think about it, the average book is less than 250 pages, but Buffet was reading six hundred to a thousand pages a day. He read everything from books to business journals about investing. He was committed, and today he is one of the richest men in the world and the top expert in the world when it comes to investing. This did not happen by luck; this happened because of his strong habit of reading. Like Warren Buffet, if we commit more of our time seeking knowledge and taking action, great things will start to happen in our lives.

Great things are Gods will for all of us, but we will not receive them until we grow up. Take for instance a wealthy family that has a ten-year-old son or a daughter that wants a car. They love their child, and they will give their child anything. This wealthy family can afford a car. The reason the ten-year-old child is not driving a car is not because the family cannot afford a car, it is because the child is not mature enough to drive a car. The child has to grow up and learn how to drive, pass some tests, obtain his or her license, then they will buy their child a car. If a loving father gave his son or daughter a car at the age of ten, it could kill that son or daughter, and that father would get locked up.

When you give somebody something before, they are ready, you hurt them instead of helping them. God is not going to give you certain things until you grow up, and we grow up by reading and praying. There are certain positions God wants to elevate us to but we are not mature enough. God wants to make us leaders, as the saying goes, leaders or readers and readers or leaders. In order for us to be the leaders God has destined us to be, it is important that we constantly read. Look at some of the great leaders in the Bible.

Exodus 2:11 says, "One day, after Moses had grown up, he went out to where his own people were and watched them at their hard labor." Notice the scripture didn't say after Moses had become older, or after Moses had come of age. The scripture says after Moses had grown up. See, growing old is mandatory but growing up is optional. As stated before, you grow up by reading, praying, and meditating. You can watch TV all day, and you will still grow old, but you will not grow up. You can be seventy years old and still be immature. But when Moses grew up, the first thing he did is that he noticed the hurt and oppression that was going on around him. Moses grew up as Pharaoh's grandson. He was given the name Moses by Pharaoh's daughter, but when he grew up, he noticed that the way he was raised was wrong. When he grew up, he identified with who he truly was, and that was a Hebrew regardless of how he was raised. When he grew up, he noticed what was wrong with society, and he instantly tried to fix it.

When a person grows up by reading good books, they start to notice that the way they were raised could have been wrong. A person's parents can be racist, but when that son or daughter grows up by reading good books, they start to realize that the way they were raised was wrong. They start to learn about the horrors and evils of bigotry, systematic racism, and systematic oppression. That's why when children go to college, some people claim that their children are being radicalized, but the truth is that these children are being educated, these children are starting to grow up and mature. The result of that education is that their eyes are opened, causing them to want to fight against injustice.

A person could be raised in a home by a sexist father. A person could be raised in a home by parents who think that poverty is inescapable and that a black person can never succeed in America. In each of these cases, just like Moses, when the children grow up by reading, they start to see that the way they were raised was wrong and they start to take action to improve their lives and the lives of others. The sad thing is that there are children who never grow up. They just grow old and continue the cycles of racism and sexism that was taught by their parents, grandparents, and ancestors.

Also, when a person grows up just like Moses, they start to identify with who they really are. Even though Moses was raised in the palace, he realized that the people being persecuted were Hebrews, and he identified with who he truly was. When you start to read, study, and live, you find out what resonates with you. You find out what you are called to do. You might have grown up in a racist household, but because you read about social justice and racism, you might want to become an elected official that helps pass laws to dismantle racist policies. You might have grown up in a poor household where you were told that a black person can never make it in this world, but you start reading about successful black entrepreneurs, and you grow up to become a millionaire and give hundreds of African Americans good paying jobs. You might have grown up in a house with a sexist father, but you start reading about women in business and politics who made history and you grow up to become the first female mayor of your city. When you read, you start to broaden your horizons and see possibilities because life is much bigger, grander, and fuller than what our individual experiences as children have taught us.

Mark Manson, the author of the *New York Times* bestselling book *The Subtle Art of Not Giving a F@ck* said that he gave himself a fifty-day challenge. It was not a challenge to post one of his favorite songs every day for fifty days. He gave himself the challenge of reading fifty non-fiction books in fifty days. He said it changed his life. Tony Robbins who is to many the world's greatest and most successful life coach or motivational speaker, said as a young man, he decided he was going to read a book a day. He said he did not quite reach his goal of reading a book a day, but by the time he was seventeen, he had read over seven hundred books. And by the time he was nineteen, he had read over a thousand books, mostly on psychology and self-development. Ask yourself how many people you know that have read a thousand books in their life time.

When it comes to reading, if you read a book one time, you have only read that book for entertainment purposes. It takes reading a great book from a great author several times to even get the gist of it. Maya Angelou said that she has read the *Seat of the Soul* ten times. Joe Dudley says he reads *Think and Grow Rich* every six months. You can read a book one time, and that book will change your life, but if you continue to read that book, you will see sustained change and growth. Reading a great book is just like watching a movie. How many people have only watched their favorite movie one time? Not many; most people watch their favorite movie over and over again. Whether your favorite movie is *Friday*, *New Jack City*, *Scarface*, *Star Wars*, *Rocky*, or *When Harry Met Sally*, you have watched that movie plenty of times.

When you are watching a great movie, it takes watching the movie several times to understand it. Like the *Godfather 1* and *2*; you have to watch those movies several times to understand the power plays in those movies and how they relate to real life. When you are in the midst of a setback, it is important that you go back to some of the books that have had the greatest impact on your life (assuming that you are a reader). The book can be the Bible or it can be particular books inside the Bible, like the book of proverbs or the book of psalms. The book could be *Think and Grow Rich*, *The Power of Positive Thinking*, *Rich Dad Poor Dad*, *Think and Grow Rich: A Black Choice*. It does not matter what the book is if the book has resonated with you and helped you in the past. It is important that you study the book when you are in the midst of a setback, and you will find new insight and encouragement to help you turn that minor setback into a major comeback.

CHAPTER 14:

GIFTS

The next step in turning a minor setback into a major comeback is recognizing and utilizing your gifts. Michael Jordan was rated by ESPN the greatest athlete of all time ahead of Babe Ruth and Muhammad Ali. People say Michael Jordan was a great athlete, but the truth is he was not the greatest athlete; he was the greatest basketball player ever, and because he was so great at basketball, he was named the greatest athlete ever. Michael Jordan was not a great baseball player. It has been proven that he's not a great golfer, which is a sport. He had a hard time beating the Detroit Pistons because they were so physical. From that alone, you can infer that he would not have been a great football player.

If Michael Jordan played baseball his whole life and tried his hardest, he might have been a decent pro, but he would not have been the greatest of all time. Even in basketball, Michael Jordan won three slam dunk contests. He was one of the greatest dunkers of all time. He participated in the three-point contest and finished next to last. In his first few years in the NBA, he was not a great three-point shooter, but he did not focus on three-point shooting; he focused on driving to the basket and mid-range jump shots.

Steph Curry is the greatest three-point shooter of all time, but he does not dunk the ball much. He is a terrible dunker. He has won three-point contests, but he has no chance of winning a dunk contest. He focuses on shooting three pointers. If basketball was all dunking, he would not even be a pro. Shaquille O'Neal, Wilt Chamberlain, and Kareem Abdul Jabber did not shoot three pointers. At the time of this writing Kareem is the all-time leading scorer in NBA history. He did not shoot three pointers. He shot the sky hook. He was not a great shooter or a great dribbler, but he has six championships, and he has six MVPS, more than anybody who has ever played basketball.

My point is that we need to focus on our strengths and what makes us unique. Because in the midst of a setback, there will be times that you will have to depend on your gifts and unique talents to make your comeback, and if you do not know what your gifts are, your comeback will be unlikely. For example, your feet are made for walking and running; have you ever tried to walk with your hands? It's possible to walk with your hands, but you will never get as far and get there as fast as walking with your feet because your feet were made for walking. Have you ever tried to eat with your feet? It might be possible, but it is much more difficult than eating with your hands because your hands were made to eat with.

The reason a lot of us are not successful at life or successful at turning our minor setbacks into major comebacks is because we try to do things that we are not made to do and don't have the talent to do. And we ignore or do not know what we are good at. Most of us are like the foot trying to be the hand or Steph Curry trying to dunk. Most of us are like Shaq trying to shoot threes or free throws. Most of us are like Michael Jordan playing baseball, and we wonder why we keep striking out in life and can't make it out the minor leagues of life. We wonder why we keep experiencing setbacks that we cannot turn into comebacks.

It is because we are doing things we are not called to do, and we are doing things we are not gifted to do. We might have the education to do it, but even people with education usually choose their majors when they are very young, and at that age, we do not have the self-awareness or the life experience to know what we are called and gifted to do. People need to get alone, pray, meditate, read, and self-reflect so that they can find out what they are good at. It might take some time, but when you find out what you are gifted at and what your purpose in life is, it is worth everything.

Jesus said for this reason I have come; he knew what he was called to do. Tom Brady is considered the greatest football player of all time; do you think he would have been a great offensive lineman? Of course not, he is too frail; he would get injured. Do you think he would be a great running back? Of course not, he is too slow. But he is the greatest football player of all time because he did what he was great at. Floyd Mayweather is undefeated in boking because he knows what he is good at it. He is not a strong puncher for a professional boxing champion; as a matter of fact, some boxing experts consider him a weak puncher, but he has the greatest defense ever, and he is the quickest; therefore, he is undefeated. The same thing with Ali. He was considered a weak puncher for a heavyweight. Ali did not have the punching power of a Tyson or Forman, but he had quick feet, and he could rope a dope. Ali did what he was great at and because of that, people consider him the greatest.

Look at Michael Jackson. He was a great entertainer and a great singer. His voice was not as strong, and he was not as good of a singer as say, Luther Vandross. He could not play multiple instruments and was not as good of a musician as Prince. What he could do better than anybody was entertain and dance and make songs that make you groove. He focused on his strengths, and he became the best ever. The same with Prince. He did not have the best voice. He focused on sensuality and playing instruments, and he became great.

Look at Sade. She does not try to dance like Tina Turner. She focuses on what she does best. Beyoncé does not try to sing like Pattie La Belle and Anita Baker. She entertains, dances, and does what she does best. Life is hard enough if you use your gifts but it's even harder for most people who choose to do what they are not good at or do not know what they are good at. When professional setbacks hit people who are working in an area they are not gifted at, they hardly ever make a comeback.

What if T.D. Jakes never accepted his call to the ministry? What if T.D. Jakes never would have preached and decided to become a businessman instead? How many people's lives would be different? What if Martin Luther King Jr. would never have become involved in the Civil Rights Movement but instead accepted a professorship at a University in Boston? How would our lives be different? What if Moses would have remained Pharaoh's grandson and stayed in his grandfather's palace instead of challenging Pharaoh? What if David would have stayed a shepherd instead of becoming king? What if Obama would have accepted a job as a corporate attorney instead of entering politics? What if Jesus would have never gone to the Cross? What if Michael Jordan decided to play baseball instead of basketball? What if Jay-Z kept selling drugs instead of rapping? What if Thomas Edison would have given up on the light bulb after he failed 9,999 thousand times? What if Detroit Red would have gone back to the streets instead of becoming a Muslim? What if Harriet Tubman would have never ran way and joined the Underground Railroad? What if Abraham Lincoln would have given up on politics once he lost his bid for Congress? What if George Washington was scared of King George the Third and the red coats and never fought in the Revolutionary War? How would our lives be different? I can tell you for certain that our lives would be worst off if these individuals did not use their talents and gifts.

The 80/20 principle is that 80 percent of your results come from 20 percent of your effort. So, we should maximize that 20 percent that produces 80 percent of the results. That 20 percent is what we do well and what we enjoy doing. When you do what you do well and what you enjoy, you will be successful, and money will follow. As the saying goes, make your vocation your vacation, and you will never have to work a day in your life. It's a shame that 80 percent of people die without ever doing the thing they were born to do, and 20 percent find out what they were born to do and do it. These 20 percent are the ones that have changed the world for the better. This is why it is so important that we find our unique talents and gifts.

The Dead Sea in the Middle East receives fresh water, but it has no outlet, so it does not pass the water out. It receives beautiful water from the rivers, and the water goes stale. I mean it just goes bad. And that why it's called the Dead Sea because it receives and does not give. And we are made the same way. We receive, and we must give. In the end, generosity is the best way to become more and more joyful. When you don't use your gifts, you are like the Dead Sea, you become stale. Suppression equals depression. When it comes to gifts, you either use them or you lose them.

Mathew 10:8 says, "Heal the sick, cleanse the leaper, raise the dead, cast out devils, freely you have received freely give." See when you give your gifts, miraculous things happen. Pharaoh and his army were chasing Moses and the children of Israel. Pharaoh's army was behind Moses, and the Red Sea was in front of them. Moses was facing a serious setback. In the midst of his setback, Moses cried to God and said, "Lord, save us." God responded by saying, why cry out to me, use what I have given you. When Moses used his gift, which was his rod, miraculous things happened. When Moses used his God-given gift, which was his rod, his setback was turned into a comeback.

A lot of us are like Moses, we are crying out and praying to God in the midst of our setbacks to make us successful, and God is saying the same thing to us he said to Moses, why cry to me, what have I given you? It is time for us to use our gifts. Think if Moses would never have used his rod, the children of Israel would have either drowned in the Red Sea or they would have been captured by Pharaoh and his army and returned to slavery. Moses was a leader and because he used his gift in the midst of a setback, the people that were following him were blessed.

We are all leaders, whether we are leading our children, families, companies, or communities. When we use our gifts, the people that follow us will be blessed. Also, when you use your God-given gifts, miraculous things happen. Martin Luther King and so many others used their gifts to fight oppression, fight for social justice and civil rights, and miraculous things happened. Barack Obama used his gift of speaking and moved forward in faith, and a miraculous thing happened. Something most people thought was impossible, and a lot black people think it is just as big of a miracle as the splitting of the Red Sea, the raising of the dead, or the healing of the sick, which is a black man becoming president. Most black people, including myself, never thought they would see that in their lifetime.

The Wright Brothers used their gift, and a miraculous thing happened, people learned how to fly. Henry Ford used his gift, and a miraculous thing happened, people could travel faster than twenty horses. Edison used his gift, and a miraculous thing happened, people could communicate with other people without being in the same vicinity as the other person. People thought it was impossible, but the telephone was invented. Notice all of these people: Moses, Jesus, the disciples, Martin Luther King Jr., Obama, the Wright Brothers, Henry Ford, and Thomas Edison were severely criticized for using their gifts. So, know that you will be criticized, doubted, or considered crazy for using your unique gifts, but you should never let the naysayers deter you if you want to turn your minor setback into a major comeback.

CHAPTER 15:

PERFECTING YOUR GIFT

The next step in turning a minor setback into a major comeback is refining and perfecting your gift. In Russell Conwell's famous book *Acres of Diamonds*, Russell tells the story of a man named Al Hafed, who lived on the bank of the river Indus. He had a nice farm with orchards and gardens, excess cash, a beautiful wife, and children. He was wealthy because he was content. Then an old priest visited him, and one night related how the world was, including the formation of all the rocks, the earth, the precious metals, and stones. He told the farmer that if he had a few diamonds, he could have not merely one farm, but many. The farmer listened. Suddenly, he wasn't that happy with what he had thus far acquired in life.

He sold his farm and went traveling in search of diamonds across Persia, Palestine, and Europe. A couple of years later, what money he had was gone and he was wandering around in rags. He finally killed himself by jumping in the sea.

The man who had bought the farmer's land was another story. One day while watering his animals in the stream that ran through the property, he noticed a rock in the watery sands. It was a diamond. In fact, it was one of the richest diamond finds in history; the mine of Golconda would yield not just one or two but acres of diamonds.

We are just like that farmer; we are sitting on acres of diamonds and do not realize it. If that farmer realized that he was living on acres of diamonds, he would be rich, and his life would have turned out very different. If we realize we are living on acres of diamonds, our lives will turn out different also. The reason that the farmer did not realize he was living on acres of diamonds is because unrefined diamonds look like regular rocks. It takes work to refine the diamonds and make them shine. We have gifts, but as long as they are not refined, we will not shine.

These gifts can make us happy and financially secure, but we don't put in the work to refine these gifts. That is why the majority of people live their lives on acres of diamonds and don't realize it. That's why the majority of people who face a setback never turn it into a comeback because they have not taken the time to refine their gifts. Therefore, they don't have the adequate skills to turn their minor setbacks into major comebacks, especially in their careers.

All of the people you admire and call successful had to work hard to refine their gifts in order for their gifts to shine. Whether it was T.D. Jakes with preaching, Jordan with basketball, Jay-Z with rapping, or Obama with politics. They all have God-given gifts, but they had to work to refine their gifts. As a matter of fact, when people first heard T.D. Jakes preaching, I don't think anybody thought he would be the most powerful preacher in our nation. When people first heard Jay-Z rap on the Hawaii Sofi record, I don't think anybody thought he would be the greatest rapper of all time. When people first heard Obama speak and when he lost to Bobby Rush, I don't think anybody thought he would be president.

Each of these individuals listed above worked on their gifts, and that work made them great. That's how they were able to turn their minor setbacks into major comebacks. Just like you can't sell unrefined diamonds because they don't shine, therefore nobody wants to buy them. The reason you can't make money off your gifts, the reason you are not shining, is because your gifts are unrefined.

A diamond is nothing but a rock that is put under intense pressure. That intense pressure and the heat the diamonds are subjected to is called the refining process. Your setbacks actually help you refine your gifts. When T.D. Jakes was preaching to imaginary people, when he was a child, that was the refining process for his gifts. When T.D. Jakes only had ten people in his congregation, but he was preaching to those ten like it was ten thousand people, that was the refining process for his gift. When the closing of the plant that T.D. Jakes worked at caused him to be unemployed, and he started preaching full time, that was the refining process of his gift.

I am sure when T.D. Jakes faced the setback of losing his job, it seemed like it was a curse, but in fact it was a blessing. Before T.D. Jakes lost his job, he had a small church. After he lost his job at the plant, he was forced to concentrate all his energy into preaching full time, and that is when his church started to grow. T.D. Jakes faced a minor setback by being fired from his job, but he turned it into a major comeback that ended up helping the lives of millions of people through his ministry.

Mark Manson in his book *The Subtle Art of Not Giving a F@ck*, said, "When Pablo Picasso was an old man, he was sitting in a café in Spain, doodling on a used napkin. He was nonchalant about the whole thing, drawing whatever amused him in that moment. Some woman sitting near him was looking on in awe. After a few moments, Picasso finished his coffee and crumpled up the napkin to throw it away as he left. The woman stopped him. Wait, she said can I have that napkin you were just drawing on I will pay you for it. Sure, Picasso replied Twenty thousand dollars. "The woman's had jolted back as if he had just flung a brick at her. What it took you like two minutes to draw that." "No ma'am Picasso said." It took me over sixty years to draw this." He stuffed the napkins in his pocket and walked out the café."

Picasso had been honing his skills for sixty years, and that, combined with his talent, is what made him great. The reason why Picasso was so successful is that he found out what he was good at and then he worked hard to improve his talent. Some people have jobs and thank God for a job, but that job is not utilizing their particular skills and talents. Then they wonder why their job or career is not fulfilling. They wonder why they are not making the progress that they desire. Well, life is hard and competitive, and it is hard to become your best and reach your goals in a job or a career that your skills and gifts cannot be utilized in. In this case, you have a job and the J.O.B. stands for just over broke, and that's how you will live the rest of your days if you don't find a career that utilizes your unique skills and gifts. Even if that career pays less than the one you are in now, you will be more fulfilled because you are doing what you love. And you will rise to the top quicker when you do what you love because you will have the energy and passion to overcome the setbacks that come with every profession and turn them into comebacks.

Think about the parable of the brick layers. Three brick layers are asked, "What are you doing?" The first says, "I am laying bricks."

The second says, "I am building a church."

The third says, "I am building the house of God."

The first bricklayer has a job. The second has a career. The third has a calling. The scripture talks about a brick layer named Nehemiah. He had a job as the king's cup bearer, but his passion and calling was to rebuild the wall of Jerusalem. He quit a secure prestigious comfortable job in order to pursue his passion, and he faced a lot of opposition for it. But it was his vision and ultimately, he was successful.

A career is what you are paid for, but a calling is what you are made for. You have to have a job or a career to pay your bills until you step into your calling or find out what you are good at. Jesus's career was that of a carpenter, but his calling was to be the Messiah. Notice Jesus did not have the career path of religious leaders of his day; he did not attend school to be a religious leader. He did not go to the school of the prophets; he did not take the career path to be a Sadducee or a Pharisee. But he was called to be the greatest spiritual leader of all time nonetheless.

Don't let anybody tell you that you don't have the background to do what God has called you to do. David's job was a shepherd, but he was called to be king. Rehab was a prostitute, but her call was to be the savior of the people of God. Mary Magdalena was a prostitute, but her call was to be the first person to spread the Gospel. Peters Job was a fisherman, but his call was to be the first leader of the church and the first pope. He, like Jesus, did not have the religious training of the Pharisees and Sadducees, but that did not stop the call of God on his life. Jay-Z's job was a drug dealer's and then a rapper, but his call was to be a cultural icon and the first billionaire in hip-hop. Sean Combs's job was a party promoter, but his calling was to be a business mogul.

A great example of somebody who found out what his calling was and excelled in it is Steve Harvey. Steve Harvey said the first time he performed standup comedy was at twenty-eight years old. He won the contest. The prize was fifty dollars. When he won, he was so excited that he cried. The girl beside him said, "Why are you crying? It is only fifty dollars." He told the young lady he knew what he was going to do for the rest of his life. The young lady said it's just fifty dollars. He said, "You don't understand, I was praying to God, asking him to show me what I was supposed to do and this is it." Steve Harvey said it was October 9; he said he went the next day and quit his job. He said the decision to quit his job cost him everything he had; he lost friends, he lost family, he lost possession, he was homeless, he had to sleep in the car for three years, but he had a vision. Because Steve Harvey decided to refine his gifts, he was able to turn those minor setbacks into major comebacks.

T.D. Jakes said, "I would hate to die but never do the thing I was born to do." Yet millions of people die every day, and they never do what they were born to do. As a matter of fact, they never even find out what they are good at. A lot those who do find out what they are good at are too scared to use their gift when they find out what their gift is. We need stop trying to be something we are not gifted at. Steve Harvey says your gift is the thing you do the best with the least amount of effort.

Marie Callender worked at a dinner and the dinner was about to go out of business. The owner told Marie that he was going out of business because business was slow. Marie did not want to hear this. This was the only job she knew, and she loved her job. She told the owner of the dinner that she was going to bring in her homemade pies the next day because people loved her pies, and she asked the owner if she could sell them at the dinner. The owner sort of shrugged her off, but he allowed her to sell her pies nonetheless. The next day, slices of her pies sold out.

She had to bring in more pies, and they sold out quickly. Eventually the dinner stopped selling hamburgers and milk shakes and sold nothing but her pies because the pies were selling so good. Marie Callender owns over 120 restaurants now, and you can't go into any frozen food section in any grocery store without seeing her pies as well as other items. It looked like it was a terrible situation, but if that dinner would have never been close to going out of business, one could infer that Marie would still be working in dinners instead of being a multi-millionaire.

Marie faced a minor setback by potentially losing the job she loved, but she turned it into a major comeback by selling her pies, which she had spent years perfecting the recipe of and starting a business. She progressed to owning over 120 restaurants that employs thousands of people. Because she turned that setback into a comeback, she was able to employ thousands of people and has given joy to the millions of people that have tasted her pies. Her vision was just to work at the diner, but God used a setback in the form of a dinner she worked at potentially going out of business as a platform to expose her gift to the world and make her rich. When you work to refine your gifts, setbacks and obstacles become opportunities to use your gifts and turn those minor setbacks into major comebacks.

CHAPTER 16:

TAKE RESPONSIBILITY

The final key to turning your minor setbacks into major comebacks is to take responsibility for everything that happens in your life. Responsibility is nothing but your response to your ability. What is your response to the ability you have? You have the ability to overcome any situation, but do you use that ability? Is your response to your ability a response that empowers you to use your innate and God-given ability to overcome any situation that you are going through? Or is your response one of victimhood, where you think that you do not have the ability to overcome and somebody else is at fault for where you are at in life and therefore somebody has to save you?

Just because something is not your fault does not mean it's not your responsibility to deal with it. Responsibility is a sign of maturity. You may not be at fault for being knocked down, but you are responsible for getting up. You see it all the time: grandparents are not at fault for their daughters becoming pregnant or their sons getting a girl pregnant, but they take care of their grandchildren because their children are not mature enough to take responsibility for their actions. Even though the grandparents are not at fault for the situation, they still take responsibility for the situation because of their maturity. Taking responsibility for what happens in your life is one of the biggest signs of maturity. In my life, I did not feel it was fair for me to be sentenced to prison for so-called tax evasion, but I did have to take responsibility for overcoming the current situation I was in.

When it comes to taking responsibility, we need to be like the eagle. One thing about eagles is that eagles never fly away from a storm. Too often, we choose to fly away or run away from storms, whether the storm is of our own making or not. The reason eagles fly higher than any other bird is that the eagles fly toward the storm, and the fierce winds and the force of the storm propels the eagle to fly above the clouds where there is only sunshine. They go through the storm and rise above it. The greats don't run from storms or problems; they take responsibility for their problems and use the winds from the storms in their lives to rise to the next level.

Notice David did not run away from Goliath; he ran toward Goliath, and because he faced that storm called Goliath, it took him to another level. Goliath was not David's fault, but he saw it as his responsibility to handle that giant situation. Fredric Douglas did not run from his slave master; he ran to him and fought him. In turn, it gained him his freedom. He faced the storm and it elevated him from a slave to a freedman. It was not Fredrick Douglas's fault that he was born a slave, but he felt it was his reasonability to confront his master. Martin Luther king Jr. did not run from Montgomery when his house was bombed. He was like the eagle; he ran toward the storm and used the fierce winds of the storm to propel him above the clouds. He faced the storm of constant death threats and his house being bombed. Because he faced the storm, they won the Montgomery bus boycott, and it elevated him from an unknown small-town preacher to the face of the Civil Rights Movement. Segregation was not his fault, racism was not his fault, but he and so many others felt it was their responsibility to deal with it.

The amazing thing about dealing with problems is that problems are just like bullies, and when you deal with them, you find out they are not that tough at all. You actually find out that problems are kind of good for you. From our limited three-dimensional perspective, we cannot really know what is good or bad for us. We can perceive what feels good or what feels bad, at the moment but, we cannot always tell what is really good or bad for us. As mentioned before, giving birth to a baby feels bad. Giving birth is the most uncomfortable and painful thing most women will go through, but even though the process of giving birth feels bad, the process of giving birth is really good because without this process, the human race could not survive. All of us humans owe our lives to this painful process.

Some things that appear to be bad at the moment can really turn out for our good. Fifty Cent getting shot nine times and being dropped from his record label seemed like a bad thing, but it ended up being the best thing that happened to him because it made him into a bigger star. Jay-Z being turned down by every record label in New York City seemed like a bad thing at the moment, but it ended up being the best thing that happened to him because it made him become a boss. Seam Combs being fired from Uptown Records seemed like a bad thing, but it was really a good thing. Because of the firing, he started Bad Boy Records. Jesus being betrayed by Judas and crucified seemed like a bad thing, but ended up being a good thing because without the betrayal, crucifixion, and death, there would not have been a resurrection. We celebrate that day of Jesus's betrayal and crucifixion and call it Good Friday. We call it Good Friday, but it certainly did not seem like it was good at the time.

Certain things in our lives do not feel good at the time, but they are good for us. They are not preferred, but they are good for us. The pressure in your life that you think has come to crush you will actually make you stronger if you take responsibility for it. Consider somebody who is in great shape and loves to work out, somebody with a chiseled body. They have muscles, but they have developed those muscles from lifting weights, from resisting pressure. The thing is that it is pressure that develops those muscles that everybody admires.

It's amazing that we admire the muscles of the person who is in great shape, but we don't want to go through the process of being pressured by weights. In order for the person's muscles to keep gaining strength, the person has to increase the amount of weight. They might start off bench pressing 98 pounds, then 120, then 180, then 250, then 280. In order for the muscles to continue to grow, they have to add more pressure. My point is, it is not the weight that makes the body builder strong, it's the fact that they push back and resist the weight that makes the body builder strong. Imagine if the bodybuilder was to just sit there and let the 280-pound weight crush his or her chest; it would do them no good, but because of their resistance, they gain strength.

We gain mental, emotional, and spiritual strength the same way by resisting problems, solving problems, and pushing against pressure. When we take responsibility for where we are at in our lives, we start to see the pressures and setbacks that come into our lives, as opportunities for growth. We see them as weights that will develop our spiritual, mental, and emotional muscles in order to help us not only to go to the next level but grow to the next level.

When it comes to gold, gold is valuable but it does not start off looking shiny. It is found in the dirt and the mud of the Earth. It starts off in an ore mixed in dirt, rock, and mud of the Earth. Then it goes through the fiery furnace. The rock, dirt, and mud are burned off and the gold remains. The 14k, the 18k, and the 24k is based on the purity of the gold. The 14k has been through the fire, but there are still quite a few impurities left. The 18k has been through the fiery furnace longer than the 14k, so it has a lot of its impurities of rock, mud, and earth burned off, but it still has some impurities left. The 24k Gold has been through the fire longer than the 14k and 18k; its impurities are burned off. The gold is so pure that the master refiner can see himself in the reflection of the gold.

God is the master refiner, and he will keep us in the fiery oven until he sees himself in our reflection. God will keep us in the fiery furnace until we are loving like him, forgiving like him, faithful like him, and powerful like him. It might not feel good or seem good when you are going through the fire at the time. You might feel like you have been in the fire for too long, but God has destined you to shine like 24k gold, not 14k; that's why you have been going through the fire for so long.

When you start to take responsibility for your life while going through the fire, when you refuse to blame God while you are in the fire, when you refuse to blame your unloving mother or your absentee father, when you refuse to blame your abusive husband or uncle, when you refuse to blame your unfaithful spouse, you will start to see major progress. True enough, it could be all of these aforementioned people's fault that you are in the situation that you are in, but it is your responsibility to come out of it better. When you decide you will take full responsibility for your life, I promise you that you will be able to turn your minor setbacks into major comebacks.